A READER'S COMPANION TO THE CONFUCIAN *ANALECTS*

Henry Rosemont, Jr.

Original hardbound and e-book editions published on demand by

Palgrave Macmillan

2012

Copyright © 2012 Henry Rosemont, Jr.

All rights reserved.

ISBN-13: 978-0-8248-5144-6

Designed and Produced by Samantha Healy

Print-ready files supplied by the author

COVER

Yuan Dynasty: Confucius annotating the classics and conversing with his students. By WangZhenpeng (fl. 1315).

Distributed by University of Hawai'i Press
www.uhpress.hawaii.edu

Lest anyone think the Confucian junzi *ideal of the exemplary person belongs only to China or the distant past, they need only look into the life and writings of the person to whom this book is most respectfully and affectionately dedicated,*

NOAM CHOMSKY

TABLE OF CONTENTS

	Acknowledgments	vii
	Preface	viii
1	What Does it Mean to be a Confucian?	2
2	Approaching the *Analects*: Is it a Book?	6
3	How Do You Spell Chinese?	15
4	The Language of the *Analects*	18
5	Terms, Concepts and Concept Clusters	24
6	The Students	30
7	The Master	37
8	On Knowing	42
9	Reading the *Analects*: Is What it Says True?	51
10	Roles, Families, and Society	58
11	Ancestor Veneration	65
12	Rituals and Spiritual Cultivation	71
13	Summary Suggestions	79
14	A Bibliographical Essay	84

APPENDIX I   95

Wade-Giles – Pinyin Conversion Table

APPENDIX II   100

Concordance of 30 Key Philosophical Terms
in the *Analects*

APPENIDIX III   107

The Students: A Finding List

ACKNOWLEDGMENTS

I am in the first instance grateful to the many undergraduate and graduate students and faculty both in the United States and China that it has been my privilege to teach the *Analects* in classes, seminars, workshops and institutes over the course of forty years. I have learned much from them, and they have been a constant source of stimulation to my thinking. Three esteemed colleagues and cherished friends read the penultimate draft of this work, and the final product is much, much richer and less error-laden for their efforts, for which I am highly grateful: Roger Ames of the University of Hawai'i, Marthe Chandler of Depauw University, and Michael Nylan of the University of California, Berkeley.

As always, my deepest debt is to my wife JoAnn Rosemont, simultaneously my biggest fan and sharpest critic, which makes her such a splendid editor and proofreader; without whom, not.

PREFACE

The major purpose of this little book is to make it easier for you the reader to come to terms with, and profit from one that is even smaller in the original, the *Analects*, which is made up of a number of statements of, by, and about Confucius, the Latinized rendering of the name of China's most famous thinker. Further on I shall have much to say about that book, but first need to say a few things about this one.

It is intended basically as a preface or prolegomenon to the *Analects* rather than a synopsis of its contents. Perhaps best construed as a tool: I have put together a series of comments, hints, finding lists and suggestions to aid readers in coming to their own interpretation of the book, necessary if it is to enrich and possibly transform their philosophical and/or religious orientations. The 511 little "sayings" which comprise the book have spoken to countless thousands across the ages, but they have not said the same things even to all readers within a single time period, let alone over the course of two millennia, in very different cultural circumstances.

There are a number of reasons for the many and varied readings of the text. Virtually every saying in it is multivocal, and they are not arranged in any easily discernible logical order. It is not a book that must or even should be read from beginning to end, for it wasn't written that way, and we aren't sure of who the "authors" ("scribes") were. Nor do we know why later editors assembled the text as they did, and we don't know who they were, either. In sum, the *Analects* must be approached differently than most books; to savor its richness the reader must engage with it *deliberately*.

This *Companion* attempts to guide the readers' approaches and engagement with the text through the provision of supplementary background materials, language analyses, finding lists, and a number of methodological suggestions for interacting with it; it is *not* an attempt to tell the reader what the text "really" says. Of course I will at times proffer my interpretation of materials – especially having to do with matters of language and translation -- but I hope these will be fairly obvious to the reader. After forty years of teaching the *Analects* as well as co-translating it I have become convinced that all efforts to impose a be-all and end-all interpretation on it are misguided for fully appreciating what it has to offer, and counterproductive for understanding how complex and complicated a person Confucius was. Even a cursory first reading of the book should show fairly clearly that while he was a highly original thinker and visionary, he was much more concerned to help his students find a humane path in life rather than describing his own idea of what the path was like in detail.

Throughout the present work I will remind readers of the importance of responding actively rather than passively to and with the text. At times this will require a good deal of effort, for such active reading is itself a key dimension of the Confucian persuasion; it is a major practice in the process of personal cultivation, having certain qualities akin to several contemplative spiritual disciplines, although distinct from them. Such discipline requires absorption in the text, proactively engaging it purposively, and learning how to read it indirectly as well as directly.

To underscore the seriousness with which Confucians attend to reading I will occasionally quote briefly the most famous of the Song Dynasty (960-1279 CE) neo-Confucian philosophers Zhu Xi on the importance thereof, beginning here, from the translation by Daniel Gardner:

> There is layer upon layer [of meaning] in the words of the sages. In your reading of them, penetrate deeply. If you simply read what appears on the surface, you will misunderstand. Steep yourself in the words; only then will you grasp their meaning.

Neither Zhu Xi nor I want to suggest that the Chinese graphs which comprise the *Analects* in the original are no more than a congeries of Rohrschach blots; not every interpretation of the text is equally valid, and in subsequent chapters I will be taking up briefly the highly attenuated sense in which Confucianism may be accounted an "ism" even though not an ideology, and hence different from other "isms" in form and thrust as well as content.

Finally, some cues are proffered for assisting the reader in coming to appreciate the religious dimensions of the *Analects*, because those dimensions will almost surely be difficult to see, much less appreciate at first acquaintance with the text by readers for whom the Abrahamic tradition is paradigmatic of religion. Although a number of divines both academic and ecclesiastic have claimed to find a concept of the transcendental realm of the sacred in the *Analects*, readers will probably be better served early on if they see the text as helping us to see how the secular might be made sacred. Put another way, Confucius does not seem to have ever thought about the meaning of life, but by his teaching and example provided a means by which everyone might find meaning *in* life, in the here and now. This is not an inconsequential accomplishment, and everyone can profit from learning how he did it, in the global "village" of today no less than in the earlier China in which he lived.

These, then, are the premises on which I have written this little *Companion;* if it assists the reader in appreciating the Confucian persuasion as I have come to do it will have served its purpose. Zhu Xi again:

> In reading, you must look for an opening in the text; . . . If you do not see an opening, you'll have no way to enter into it. Once you find an opening, the coherence of the text will naturally become clear.

A READER'S COMPANION TO THE CONFUCIAN *ANALECTS*

Chapter 1
WHAT DOES IT MEAN TO BE A CONFUCIAN?

Within the Western religious traditions it makes no sense to speak of Christianity before the time of Christ, nor Islam before Mohammed. Clearly, however, it does make sense to speak of Judaism before the time of Moses, and the same may be said of Confucian teachings and practices. Probably the best way to understand who Confucius was and what he did, and to appreciate why he has been the most famous human symbol of Chinese civilization for two thousand years, is to realize that much of what he advocated -- attentiveness to ritual propriety, ancestor veneration, the importance of learning, family ties, a hierarchical social order, and much more -- were all embedded in Chinese culture as much as a millennium before he was born.

To be sure, he modified significantly the cultural materials he inherited. Many ancient Chinese customs, political norms and religious practices were originally founded on supernatural beliefs which, by the time Confucius lived (551-479 BCE), were no longer being taken very seriously among reflective members of the governing elite, and no small measure of his genius lay in giving humanistic and naturalistic justifications for not altogether abandoning those customs, political rules, social norms and religious practices even when their foundational *raison d'etre* was no longer credible. I will return to this theme later (Chapters 11 and 12), but can amplify briefly here the Master's insight on this score with a quotation from the early 20th Century American philosopher George Santayana, who said "I reject wholly the dogma of the Roman Church – but rejoice in the splendor and the beauty of the Mass." Equally illustrative is the remark attributed to Karl Marx when asked why he attended Mass regularly: "Where else can you hear Bach for nothing?"

It is largely for this reason that Confucianism has never been a static system, despite numerous charges to that effect by its detractors both within and outside East Asia. Indeed, Confucianism has never really been a "system" at all, consistently undergoing change and adaptation throughout its history; one reason it is misleading to use the term "Confucianism" is that there is no word for it in the classical Chinese language (more on that below). Even its earliest heroes after the death of the Master and his immediate circle – Zisi, Mencius, Xunzi, etc. – advanced views that differed from those found in the *Analects* (and from each other); in the later Han Dynasty writers began adding a metaphysics (and a dogmatism) to the growing tradition that did not exist before; the Song Dynasty neo-Confucian re-interpretations of the texts, synthesized by the prodigious scholar Zhu Xi were deeply indebted to strong Buddhist influences and to manifold social, economic and technological changes that had changed China as well, and those re-interpretations were re-interpreted in turn during the succeeding Ming and Qing dynasties. The views of the Ming thinker Wang Yangming, for instance, are as different from those of Zhu Xi as are Plato's from Aristotle's, but they are both described as "(Neo)-Confucians." The 20th Century saw a number of efforts to reconstruct the Confucian persuasion in light of two world wars, the rise and fall of communism, and the internationalization of economic and political affairs, a process ongoing in the 21st Century, again, both in China and the West.

In this connection it bears noting that the Confucian vision was challenged from the outset by rival schools of early Chinese thought such as the Mohists, Legalists, Daoists and others. It was later eclipsed religiously by Buddhism for more than a millennium, and then, after the neo-Confucian resurgence that got underway in the 11th Century CE, was challenged again by Jesuit, Dominican and Franciscan missionaries at the very end of the 16th Century and into the 17th. With the humiliation of China that began two hundred years later by imperialist adventurers, invading armies, and Protestant missionaries from Western Europe and the United States – and later Japan and Russia – the Confucian vision was challenged yet again by Western Enlightenment ideas of individualism, equality and democracy, and still later, was eclipsed by Marxist attacks that culminated in the 1970s with the "Anti-Confucius" campaign of the Great Proletarian Cultural Revolution.

From all of these attacks Confucian teachings and practices adapted, recovered, and regained a seldom-paralleled prominence which should give pause to thinking that it is only of antiquarian interest today, and/or merely capable of providing some clues as to how contemporary Chinese leaders might think. Rather might we entertain the idea that perhaps there is something in the way of life first envisioned by Confucius that speaks not only to and for the past, but to the present as well; not only to the Chinese, but to peoples of all cultures. There is certainly a Confucian "revival" of sorts going on in mainland China today, much of it without any government support; most universities there, for example, now have schools of Confucian Studies in them, independent Confucian primary and secondary schools are growing in number throughout the country, while the government has provided funding for the establishment of Confucius Institutes around the world, numbering 350+ at present. This is not to say, however, that the Confucian persuasion should be seen as a universalizing religion or philosophy to which everyone should adhere, for a central element of the general Confucian "way" is that there are many particular human ways, and each of us must tread that way which best suits our histories, genealogies, talents and personalities, a theme to which we will return in the pages to follow.

Chapter 2

APROACHING THE *ANALECTS:*
IS IT A BOOK?

The title of this chapter might strike the reader as somewhat strange, for what else could the *Analects* be but a book? Well, it is indeed a "book," but a most atypical one (not unlike the Bible in some respects), so before addressing directly the details of the book – and what Confucius was about – the reader should have some understanding of its form, structure and historical development as a unique document.

The 511 sections which comprise the *Analects* (several of which are duplicative) were written, compiled and edited over the course of three centuries by a number of people about whom we know relatively little. We do not know who the "authors" were with any degree of certainty, nor why the later compilers and editors arranged the text we now have the way they did. The 511 "sayings" consist of fairly laconic statements Confucius is supposed to have made, or answers he gave to his students' queries. They also contain a number of statements by the students themselves, and still other statements made by we know not who, or when.

These sayings were written down on dried bamboo strips and then rolled into bundles to make a little "book" made up of a number of smaller sections. Several such "books" existed in varied forms and groupings and were in circulation for a considerable period of time before being edited into their present form approximately fifty years after the Han Dynasty (202 BCE – 220 CE) was established – i.e., almost three hundred and fifty years after Confucius died.

As Michael Nylan has recently argued, it was only during the Han that China began to become a truly manuscript culture, with reading becoming an essential ingredient of personal cultivation, taking on some of the attributes of a spiritual discipline which we will explore in later chapters. Here, however, what must be emphasized is that the lessons Confucius taught he taught *orally*; contemporary readers of the *Analects* must attempt to recapture the spirit of personal give-and-take encounters between Master and students, in the same way we should endeavor to do when reading about Socrates, especially in the early and middle dialogues. Another quote from Zhu Xi on reading is *apropos* here:

> It's best to take up the books of the sages and read them so that you understand their ideas. It's like speaking with them face to face.

Of course there were books extant in the time of Confucius, and he regularly exhorted his disciples – including his son – to read and study them, especially the *Shijing* (*Book of Odes*, also called the *Book of Songs* or *Book of Poetry*) and *Shujing* (*Book of History* or *Book of Documents*); both of which he quotes from himself. The later scholarly traditions have him writing or editing other texts which later became canonical, and definitive of the Chinese cultural tradition: *The Book of Changes, The Spring and Autumn Annals,* and the *Zuo Commentary* thereon. (He is also linked to one of the famous ritual texts, the *Records of Ritual*).

But if he was indeed responsible for assembling the "Five Classics," as these texts came to be known, he must have done so while suffering from a mild form of schizophrenia, for the five differ widely in scope, thrust, doctrines and practices, each presenting materials altogether conflicting with other materials – sometimes even from the same text.

This is another reason why it is misleading to use the term "Confucianism" as a cover term for all the personages found in the *Analects* and their successors, as if there were a core set of beliefs and practices to which everyone had to adhere in order to insure membership in the group. Quite the contrary: two centuries after the Master died, the legalist thinker Hanfeizi described eight factions of "Confucians" with divergent views and practices, not having a great deal in common save for tracing their lineage back to Confucius.

Moreover, it is important to note again that there is no Chinese graph for which "Confucianism" is a translation. *Ru* 儒, the term used by Hanfeizi and everyone else basically meant simply "classicist," – the learning of the literati. The term does, however, go back even further in time, to the Shang Dynasty, and probably meant something like "scribe." Several centuries after the death of Kongqiu or Kongzi – i.e., Confucius -- the *ru* came to have significant access to the throne at the Han court and since that time the graph has taken on the additional meaning of "scholar-official," but without losing the sense of "classicist."

For all these reasons today's readers should not seek an "orthodox" reading of the *Analects*. The text, although uniformly read and revered, did not itself achieve full canonical status until well over a millennium after achieving its present form, when the interpretation of the text by Zhu Xi became "orthodox," in that it became a basis of the imperial civil service examinations for over seven hundred years. (But even then successive governments never forbade private academies from providing "unorthodox" readings of the texts.)

Thus, just as with other schools of thought in classical China, early Confucian teachings and practices are probably best understood in terms of lineages, beginning with the Master himself and his own students, some of whom later took on students themselves, and continuing, with the dominant pattern of scholarship not being book learning, but formal and informal discussion among and between a group of learners centering around a talented teacher. Recapturing this sense of oral learning from reading the *Analects* we have today is not easy, but is surely worth a try.

Returning now to the text as a physical document, greatly complicating efforts to more definitively establish a chronology for its composition and editing is the fact that in 213 BCE a massive "Burning of the Books" took place during the reign of

Qin Shi Huangdi – he of terra cotta tomb soldier fame – with many texts extant at the time not surviving the bibliographic holocaust except in special libraries, themselves destroyed in turn during the years of civil war that followed shortly after the emperor's death and the fall of the Qin and he rise of the Han.

In their present form the sections of the *Analects* have been gathered together into twenty short "books" with the arrangement thereof seemingly arbitrary much of the time. Several topics are discussed in each little book – not consecutively for the most part – and are also discussed in other books, but one must look with great care to ascertain a relationship among and between them, and in a number of cases no such relationship can be found. There are, however, clusters of concerns in each book that it will be helpful for the reader to know when searching for a particular theme, or retrieving an analect. They are as follows:

Book 1 -- Some Basic Concepts/Terms
Book 2 -- *Xiao* (Family Reverence), Governance
Book 3 -- *Li* (Rituals & Ritual Propriety)
Book 4 -- *Ren* (Consummate Person/Conduct)
Book 5 -- The Master's Comments on the Students
Book 6 -- The Master's Comments on the Students
Book 7 -- Autobiographical; Transmitting the Past
Book 8 -- Steadfast Commitment to the Dao (Way)
Book 9 -- Contextless Sayings of Confucius
Book 10 -- Formal Behavior of Confucius
Book 11 -- See Books 5 and 6
Book 12 -- On Governance
Book 13 -- On Governance

Book 14 -- Evaluations of Historical Personages
Book 15 -- More contextless sayings of Confucius
Book 16 -- Miscellany
Book 17 -- Miscellany
Book 18 -- Unusual People, Recluses, etc.
Book 19 -- Sayings of the Students
Book 20 -- Miscellany

The present Books 4 through 8 are generally agreed to be the oldest strata of the text in terms of containing statements the scribe purportedly actually heard Confucius make. For some scholars Books 3 and 9 belong in this group as well. Books 1 and 2 come next, followed by 11– 15, with books 15 – 18 next in turn, with Books 10, 19 and 20 generally agreed to be the most recent. Another traditional division of the text has been into an early Book made up of little books 1 – 10, with the remaining 10 making up a later text, the two of them being combined at a later date. (This latter division, however, is not of much practical use in the interpretation of textual passages today.)

In sum, like the other great spiritual teachers of antiquity -- Socrates, Jesus and the Buddha -- Confucius never wrote anything, or at least is not known to have written anything that has come down to us, and thus we must rely on the reports of others as to what he said, some of whom were not yet born when he died in 479 BCE. Those sayings were still later collected, arranged and re-arranged in ways that defy the imposition of a single logical order on them.

These and a number of related factors have contributed

significantly to making the *Analects* a unique text, but the difficulties of ascertaining its origins and development have been long known and a part of the Chinese intellectual heritage, and hence have not been a hindrance to the seventy-odd generations of Chinese who studied the text intensively, and almost invariably memorized it. The text was quite literally set in stone in the 2nd Century CE, and, as noted earlier, it served as the basis for the Chinese civil service examinations for over seven centuries until they were abolished in 1905.

The first Western translation of the *Analects* was published in Latin as *Confucius Sinarum Philosophus* in 1687. It and subsequent sinological materials were read and discussed with great interest in Europe by missionaries and theologians, but were for the most part ignored by philosophers until very recently. A notable exception to this neglect was the great German thinker Gottfried Wilhelm Leibniz, who wrote a *Discourse on the Natural Theology of the Chinese* in 1716, the last year of his life, in which he argued at length for the compatibility between Confucianism and Christianity, because both were compatible with his own philosophy.

There are a number of English-language translations of the *Analects* in common circulation today, many of them competently done. In the bibliographic appendix at the end of this work I shall say something about them, but want to note now that all of my references to the text will be, unsurprisingly, to the translation I did with my dear friend and collaborator

Roger Ames: *The Analects of Confucius: A Philosophical Translation* – hereafter A&R. He and I have both used this work in our courses and seminars for many years, as have a large number of our colleagues, from whose comments we have profited greatly, as we have profited equally from the responses of our students. (And I have profited equally from collaborating with Ames over many years.)

We subtitled our work "A Philosophical Translation" to underscore first, that as philosophers we believe it is necessary to weigh the merits of the views under examination and not merely record them; if we did not believe a great many of those views might claim the allegiance of many people of intelligence and good will today we would not have bothered translating and presenting them to the English-speaking public. Historians and philologists productively undertake translations without comment on their relevance or truth, but philosophers must address those and related matters. All the more have we been comfortable with our overall approach to the translation because an important dimension of our interpretation of it is that the Confucian tradition has always adapted to changing circumstances over generations.

We do not believe it is possible to translate without interpreting. Some translators believe they can do so, but I am not one of them, nor is Ames. Hence we believed it was necessary that we make explicit in our Introduction to the translation the assumptions on which we based our readings of the text, our views of the nature of the languages used in the translation — English and classical Chinese – and our views of the nature of human language more generally, and the uses to which it may be put. As my views on these issues have not changed greatly since our translation was published, there is no need for a detailed rehearsal of them in this *Companion*; many issues of language remain, however, and it will be necessary to consider those issues as they assist readers in evaluating other translations and interpretations of the text.

Chapter 3
HOW DO YOU SPELL CHINESE?

Throughout the present work the Romanization system for transliterating Chinese terms will be *pinyin,* developed in China a decade after Liberation in 1949, and which has become standard there ever since, (Although it only became standard in Taiwan in 2008.) Most of the newer *Analects* translations use *pinyin,* as have an increasing number of Western scholars of China beginning in the mid-1970s.

But other English language translations employ another method of transliteration, the Wade-Giles system, which was also the system used by most writers on things Chinese before the late 1970s. Thomas Wade, a member of the British foreign service in China for many years, (and later the holder of the first chair in Chinese at Cambridge University), developed a Romanized transliteration system for Chinese characters in the 1860s which began as a syllabary. Modified by Herbert Giles at the turn of the century, it quickly became the accepted standard for the spelling of Chinese in China itself no less than in the English-speaking West, although other orthographies continued in use.

Neither the Wade-Giles nor *pinyin* terms make very clear to a native English speaker how they are to be pronounced much of the time; there are linguistic justifications for both systems, but these often confuse the general reader. The many characters pronounced **shirr,** for example, are spelled *shih* in Wade-Giles and *shi* in *pinyin;* **duh** becomes *te/de,* and **she** is rendered *hsi/xi.* At times the seemingly odd spellings are due to Chinese having a number of sounds that are also found in French or German but not in English: Wade-Giles *jen (* pinyin *ren)* -- which approximates English **run** in sound -- is one orthographic example, as is the inclusion in Wade-Giles of the German umlaut (e.g., ü). The common sound **jurr** is realized orthographically in Wade-Giles as *chih.* Switching to *pinyin* isn't much help here, for the latter spelling is *zhi.* (But we mustn't get angry at the Chinese for employing an orthography which is fairly counterintuitive for native English speakers, because they didn't devise it for native English speakers; they had their own 1+ billion people in mind as they constructed their alternative to Wade-Giles).

Thus today's reader of the *Analects* who wishes to befriend it must become acquainted with both Wade-Giles K'ung Tzu and the *pinyin* Kongzi no less than with the common Latinized spelling, "Confucius." They must also be attentive to punctuation and syllabication which are fairly minimal in *pinyin.* While the surname continues to be placed first, only the first of the given names is capitalized, and they are not separated by a hyphen in *pinyin*, so that the Mao Tse-tung of revolutionary days is being remembered in the history books as Mao Zedong. The *Tao Te Ching* by Lao Tzu is now the *Daodejing* by Laozi.

Initially, probably the greatest difficulty readers new to the

Analects will have is being able to distinguish the students from each other, for fully a third of the 15 most prominent of them have names rendered in *pinyin* which begin with *zi*, "Master," pronounced roughly as **dzuh.** They are Zigong (**goong**), Zilu (**loo**), Zixia (**shiah**), Ziyou (**yo**), and Zizhang (**jahng**); it should help if the reader pronounces these names aloud when encountered in the text until they become familiar, because it is very important to know specifically to whom Confucius is speaking, a subject we will take up again in Chapter 6, below.

Until the reader gets the hang of pronouncing at least approximately correct both systems of spelling, a transcription conversion table is provided (Appendix I) to help readers go from one to the other. Because Chinese is a tonal language, both Wade-Giles and *pinyin* use superscript numbers 1 through 4 to indicate whether the character is to be pronounced high and even, rising, falling then rising, or falling, respectively. But most of the time the superscripts are not given, so the beginning (and intermediate) reader of the *Analects* need not worry about pronouncing the words any more correctly than they need to be for purposes of remembering them.

Unfortunately, the Wade-Giles and *pinyin* systems do not exhaust the methods of Romanization of all English translations, which will be noted in the Bibliography at the end of this *Companion.*

Chapter 4
THE LANGUAGE OF THE <u>ANALECTS</u>

When reading a translated text it is useful to keep in mind the differences between the object and the target languages of the composition of the text(s); in this case, classical Chinese and contemporary English. There are great differences between the two, which Ames and I have discussed in detail in both the Introduction and 2nd Appendix to our translation of the *Analects*. Herein I will only sketch some major themes involving interpretation – not of the meaning of the text, but of its language.

It is first necessary to note that writing is not solely – and at times, not even mainly – a transcription of speech. No indirect discourse is speech transcribed, nor are newspaper headlines, many advertisements, and much else. This feature of language is particularly important with respect to classical Chinese, especially Confucian teachings, because of the ubiquity in the *Analects* of *zi yue* 子曰, "The Master said." In the first place, one feature of all natural (spoken) languages is their capacity to unambiguously express grammatical relations, but classical Chinese does not have this feature uniformly; absent a specific context, grammatical relations are not unambiguously expressed.

An equally important reason for not seeing classical Chinese as a transcription of speech is phonetic. There is very little direct evidence to suggest that basic *verbal* communication took place through this medium on a major scale. Nor could there be such, because the extraordinarily large number of homonyms makes it virtually uninterpretable by ear alone (without the use of binomes). A great many semantically unrelated lexical items have exactly the same phonological realization to be understood aurally, even when tonal distinctions are taken into account (and the ancient consonantal endings added). This is not to suggest a complete disconnect between the spoken and written Chinese languages at the various times that the classical texts were being written and edited. The *Book of Odes* obviously was a recording of sounds, and phonetic loan words are found early on in the written record. And *perhaps* one or two of the disciples of Confucius did place a *verbatim* quote from the Master into the text that has come down to us. But it remains that classical Chinese should not be seen as fundamentally a transcription of speech.

Originally the classical language had a number of syllabic consonantal endings which are no longer present in the modern language, but even then the number of homonyms was high, with anywhere from two to seven different graphs – with different meanings – pronounced identically. No one will understand a passage read aloud from a classical text unless they have read it earlier, and can contextualize it. Thus the language of the classical texts was fundamentally like the good little boy: primarily to be seen and not heard.

However, the several lineages that began with the teachings of Confucius were fundamentally transmitted orally, as the regular employment of "The Master said" makes clear. But much that was actually said does not seem to have been transcribed, but was rather written down later using the Chinese graphs in "sentences" which were closely related to, but not identical with those of the spoken language; somewhat akin to the relationship between spoken English and what is written in telegrams and newspaper headlines. (This is not to imply that classical written Chinese is not a powerful means of expression and communication. It is allusive throughout, can reflect strongly-felt and complex emotions in brief compass, and is often productively ambiguous.)

I also believe that classical Chinese differs in another important way that other translators have neglected or ignored: It is more an event-based than a "thing"-based language, more akin to Hebrew than to most members of the Indo-European language groupings. Ames and I have argued for this claim elsewhere, and I will not rehearse it herein, save to make the related claim that the nature of early Chinese metaphysics reflects the structural nature of the Chinese language. There is little by way of substance ontology – *"being"* – to be found in early Chinese thought, but much in the way of events, processes – *"becoming."* Many English nouns can be "verbed," to be sure, but in classical Chinese, virtually every graph can function as noun and verb, and usually as an adjective or adverb as well, which is no more than to say that apart from context the grammatical function of a Chinese term can seldom be ascertained. The resultant linguistic dynamism of classical

Chinese will thus only be captured at all well in English if verbs take pride of place in translation, and the use of gerunds made common throughout. Thus instead of "Zizhang asked about government" for 子張問政, a more dynamic translation would read "Zizhang asked about governing effectively."

It is also important to note that classical Chinese language is an analytic (uninflected) language, in that its terms are not marked for gender, number or tense; there are no cases, and originally there were no punctuation marks (although some graphs functioned as such to some extent at the time the text was edited into its present form); in other words, apart from context the syntactic status of the graphs cannot be ascertained with any precision.

The lack of markings for gender, case and number in classical Chinese deserves especial notice. The great majority of English translations in common circulation today translate the Chinese term *junzi* (君子), which is what Confucius calls his model person, as "Gentleman," with the concomitant "he" and "him" as referential pronouns. To be sure, ancient China had many of the trappings of a patriarchal society, but perhaps may not have been as oppressive to women then as it later became during the imperial period. Moreover, even if the status of women was indeed uniformly grim during the time of the early Confucians, there is evidence that they themselves were not the sexists they have all too often been portrayed as being. (A competing school of thought – the followers of Mozi – for example, sharply criticized the Confucians for according women the same familial and ritual deference as men.)

No less significant for appreciating the text today is the fact that in addition to the grammar of the language, the educational, ethical and political importance Confucius and his followers placed on model emulation, strongly suggest that *junzi* should be rendered as "Exemplary persons," with attendant "they." Especially is this so, in our view, because of the importance in the contemporary world of striving for full gender equality while yet maintaining the strong familial bonds on which Confucian ethics rests; if the Master is to be able to speak to us at all today the language we oblige him to speak should certainly not be off-putting to half of his potential audience from the start. Thus, if Confucian teachings are to remain consistent with its pedagogy, they must be re-visioned by each succeeding generation; and because the current generation (rightly) rejects sexism, there is even less justification for retaining the solely masculine flavor of older translations, and constant use of the singular.

With respect to the semantic component of the grammar, almost every graph has a multiplicity of meanings. Not infrequently the meanings are disparate -- especially when the graph has differing phonetic realizations – as for example, in the graph 樂. Pronounced *yue* the graph means "music;" pronounced *yao*, "joy," "pleasant," "happy," etc.; and pronounced *le*, it means "to enjoy." The graph 心 *xin* (originally a stylized picture of the aorta) refers to both the seat of our thoughts and of our feelings; rendering it as such in verbal form would thus be "thinking and feeling," but "heart-mind" is becoming standard as the noun form, although still making the separation; this conveys the basic sense of the term better than either term alone, and makes it a bit easier to appreciate fully by those accustomed to making a sharp distinction between the cognitive and affective dimensions of our lives and our activities.

These syntactic, semantic and phonetic properties of classical Chinese collectively contribute to giving a great many of the statements which comprise the text an initial strangeness which must be thought through, and an ambiguity about them that may defy resolution, no matter how carefully thought through. It should thus not be surprising to learn that there are over eight thousand commentaries that have been written on the *Analects*, or sections of it, over the course of the past two millennia in China, and that many of those commentaries directly contradict others. (It is also why there are so many translations of the text in English and other Indo-European languages.)

In the following chapter we will continue this discussion of the Chinese language and the importance of reader sensitivity to how and why its graphs sound, are arranged, and mean what they do, which should aid the reader measurably in evaluating the merits and demerits of the several translations of the text into English.

Chapter 5
TERMS, CONCEPTS, AND CONCEPT CLUSTERS

Every culture has a vocabulary denoting core concepts for describing, analyzing and evaluating human conduct, long ago as well as today. In contemporary English that vocabulary tends to cluster around the term "morals" and includes such other terms as "freedom," "ought," "rights," "liberty," "reason," "obligation," "choice," "dilemma," "evil," "objective/subjective," " right/wrong," "individual," "duty," and several related terms. Without these terms a discussion of moral issues could not take place. Unfortunately for any and all efforts to speed read the *Analects* for its moral insights, *none* of these terms clustered around the concept of "morals" has a close lexical equivalent in classical Chinese, and hence, in a very significant sense, Confucius should not be described as a "moral philosopher" *in the contemporary English meaning of that expression,* for imposing our current concept-cluster on his text will only eventuate in seeing him as a well-meaning preacher at best, as a muddled or hopelessly naïve thinker at worst.

It follows that the *Analects* is not a book of moral philosophy in anything like our present Western sense of moral philosophy, and we must therefore struggle to read it on its own terms without bringing ours to bear on it. This is a very difficult task, and can never be altogether successful even for scholar/translators. (Several of whom have indeed imported much of the contemporary English vocabulary into their rendering of the Chinese). But the effort is eminently worthwhile because the ethical and spiritual insights found in the *Analects* are many and profound in my opinion. Hence let us bracket the term "morals" and its attendant concept-cluster of other terms because so many of them have no close analogues in the Chinese lexicon. In this way the reader may become more open to other views of the personal and social worlds, in this case the personal and social world of Confucius. I will instead use the more general term "ethics," defining it as *the study of descriptions, analyses and evaluations of human conduct, and proffering critiques thereof.* With this definition we open ourselves to views that may be at variance with some or many of ours, and when we approach a sacred text, should therefore ask the question all people of good will should ask most fundamentally, namely, "How could a highly intelligent and thoroughly decent person accept the view of the world, and/or human beings, that are expressed in this book?"

Thus in the present case we must attend carefully at the outset to the Confucian concept cluster found in the Introduction to the A&R translation, and to read Book 1 particularly closely, because in it many of the basic philosophical and religious terms Confucius employs to describe, analyze and evaluate human conduct are presented, albeit unsystematically. Book 1 should not be read only to become acquainted with the terms in the Confucian concept cluster, of course, but it is a useful way to begin to take the text seriously.

Let me say just a bit more about concept clusters to insure that we are all on the same page with respect to how to approach books whose underlying presuppositions are different from our own, and embedded in a language equally different from our own. Even in Western culture the concept cluster of morals is fairly modern. In Chaucer's and later Medieval and Renaissance days in England, for example, the description, analysis and evaluation of human conduct employed such terms as "liegeful," "varlet," "sake," "shent," "troth," "chivalric," "boon," "soke," "sooth," "villein," "churl," and several others clustered around the concept of honour.

In the same way, Indian accounts use terms like "dharma," "samsara," "moksha," "samadhi," "karma," "Brahman," "dukkha," "maya," "atman," "avidya," and more. Now if we want to enter the ethical world of our medieval ancestors, or the worlds of Hindus and Buddhists, we must come to understand these concepts and employ correctly the terms which denote them. In just the same way, if we want to gain the insights to be obtained from the *Analects*, we must become familiar with the Confucian concept cluster centered in the term *ren*, which is translated as "authoritative" in A&R. To this end I have appended a concordance (Appendix II) for thirty basic Chinese terms of philosophical and religious import. It will be quickly noticed that virtually every one of them has several meanings, and hence readers will be well advised to back and fill when going through the text to see how a term is used and translated in different passages. The task is made a little easier for the readers of the A&R translation because the *pinyin* is always included in parentheses in the English text for the most important of the philosophical terms. Eventually the concept-cluster of the *Analects* will become familiar to the reader, but five key terms require especial consideration.

The first of these is *tian*天, uniformly translated as "heaven" (or worse, "Heaven") most of the time, and occasionally as "Nature." (It also means "sky" of course, but is seldom translated that way). The first of the missionaries to China, Matteo Ricci, allowed that *tian* could be translated as "God," although he himself coined the neologism *tian zhu*, "Heaven's Lord," which later became the only way "God" could be translated in the Roman Catholic faith. The A&R translation merely transliterated the graph, explaining in the Introduction why "Heaven" was a poor choice in our opinion because of its immediate association with the dwelling place of the departed faithful in the Abrahamic religious traditions, a concept I personally do not think Confucius ever entertained any more than he thought of anything like the God of those traditions, a claim with which most missionaries since Ricci's time – even most of his fellow Jesuits – would agree (There remain, however, a number of exceptions).

At the same time, however, there are passages in the *Analects* which seem to suggest fairly strongly that Confucius indeed attributed agency and purpose to *tian* at times, even though most of the time he did not. Thus it will probably be best for readers to go through all the passages in which *tian* occurs in order to develop their own sense of the range of meanings the term might have, in the end letting *tian* simply be *tian*, keeping in mind that some interpreters of the text wish to maintain a sense of divinity inhering in the term..

The second term requiring initial comment is *ren* 仁. As Ames and I explained in our Introduction, "authoritative" seemed the closest in English meaning for *ren*, but more recently we have come to believe "consummate conduct" more nearly captures the sense of the Chinese, at the same time admitting that the common terms employed by our fellow translators – "benevolence," "human-heartedness," "humaneness" – also capture an important (empathetic) connotation of *ren* as well, which our "consummate conduct" does not. Like *tian*, then, it is better, I now believe, to simply gloss *ren* and then simply transliterate it. If readers find the concept difficult to understand, they may draw consolation from the text itself, when it is seen just how often the students ask the Master to define the term for them.

The third graph requiring comment at the outset is *yi* 義, usually translated as "morals," or as "righteous," "righteousness." The former is not efficacious because of the other terms in the concept-cluster surrounding "morals" listed at the beginning of this chapter, and thus can lead the reader astray by imposing a very Western orientation on the text from which it will be hard to disengage. The same goes for "righteous" and "righteousness" with respect to the concept-cluster found in the Hebrew scriptures, New Testament, and the Quran: objective, external and invariant standards of conduct imposed from without, binding on all.

To my mind both of these interpretive translations impose too much of a Western orientation on the *Analects,* making it much more difficult for us to understand what Confucius might be saying to us. But "appropriate" for *yi* does not impose anywhere near as narrow a reading: we are at all times to endeavor to do what is maximally appropriate to do in the circumstances, and if we do something else, it will be inappropriate *(bu yi).* And what is appropriate – fitting, proper – ranges over all of our conduct, from issues of protocol (10.4) to paying respect to elders (1.6), from following the ruler's or parental orders to challenging them (3.19, 4.18). Indeed, it is not only our conduct, but our attitude toward that conduct that can be said to be appropriate or inappropriate, as 2.7 and 2.8 make clear.

Against this background readers may turn to the Concordance (Appendix II) for these three and other key philosophical terms in the *Analects* to begin the process of familiarization with them. The two additional key terms --*zhi* 知 "knowledge" and -*li* 禮 "rituals" – require more extensive discussion in separate chapters.

Chapter 6
THE STUDENTS

According to the record of the famous Han historian Sima Qian – written centuries after the Master's death – Confucius is supposed to have said that he had 77 students of some note (or notoriety), who were, the record has him adding, "All of exceptional ability." (Some of their abilities, as we shall see, were matched by shortcomings which the Master regularly noted bluntly in the *Analects*.) Only 22 names can be assigned to students with any certainty in the text itself, however, with another 3 or 4 possible others mentioned depending on how the context is interpreted.

They were an interesting and engaging lot, and varied greatly in their personalities and conduct; if the Legalist philosopher Hanfeizi is to be believed, several of them formed distinctive lineages of their own based on what they learned (and perhaps didn't learn) from their own teacher. Thus, becoming acquainted with them is perhaps the most important single technique that can be employed by serious readers in order to most fully understand and appreciate the remarks Confucius makes to (and about) them, and the answers he gives to their queries.

Brief biographies of the most well-known of them are given in the A&R Introduction to the *Analects,* and somewhat lengthier accounts of a number of them are given in the translations of others. It will be better for readers, however, to ignore all of these brief biographies (including ours) and construct their own on the basis of the several analects in which they appear in the text itself, because they are almost the only plausible source of our knowledge of who they were, what Confucius thought of them, and hence why he said to them what he did.

Why this knowledge is very important for interpreting the remarks of Confucius is made very clear in 11.22 with an autobiographical remark on his pedagogy, crucial for the contemporary reader to appreciate in coming to terms with a great many of the remarks he makes when conversing with his students.

> Zilu inquired, "On learning something, should one act upon it?" The Master said "While your father and elder brothers are still alive, how could you, learning something, act upon it?" Then Ranyou asked the same question. The Master replied, "On learning something, act on it." Gongxi Hua said, "When Zilu asked the question, you observed that his father and brothers are still alive but when Ranyou asked the same question you told him to act on what he learns. I am confused – could you explain this to me?" The Master replied, "Ranyou is diffident, and so I urged him on. But Zilu has the energy of two, and so I sought to rein him in."

It thus behooves the serious reader to peruse all of the analects – almost half of the text -- in which a student is named, and to make this task a little easier a Finding List for each of them mentioned three or more times is included at the end of this *Companion* (Appendix III). Even so, the reader will still have much work to do in coming to his or her own evaluation of many of the students, for Confucius sometimes praised, and sometimes faulted virtually all of them (Yan Hui being about the only exception). Zigong, for example, is given high marks in 1.15, but sarcastically put down in 14.29; Confucius says that Ranyou was surely qualified to hold political office (6.8) and excelled in statesmanship (11.3), but is then excoriated by the Master for his failures in just that area in 11.17.

At other times Confucius is surprisingly frank in his judgments of specific students, especially in Books 5, 6 and 11, but in many cases we do not know to whom he is addressing his evaluations, or why; they are simply there, and despite a great deal of calligraphic ink being used to explain these analects in a myriad of (often conflicting) commentaries, we are, in the end, left to make of them what we will.

After reading, and then re-reading all of the analects in which a particular student speaks or is described, the reader should reflect thereon, and form a tentative opinion of the kind of person overall the student appears to have been, and was judged by Confucius. Then a number of the answers the Master gives to that person's questions should be studied in order to see how they might be given an interpretation that would not be obvious on a first or quick reading.

All of this is reading actively, and is necessary for deepening one's own interpretation of the text as a whole as well as of the parts which serve as windows on ancient Chinese thinking . But at the deepest level the activity of reading must be such as to have the text also become a *mirror* of the reader's own opinions, beliefs and patterns of reasoning. A salutary intellectual (and effective) exercise, for example, is for the reader to think long and hard as to why they formed the opinion of a particular student that they did indeed form, tentatively or with greater assurance. In other words, given that the evidence for all the students is more or less conflicting — again, Yan Hui is the exception – why did *these* accounts of the student weigh more heavily on *me* (the reader) than *those* accounts? Why might we be inclined to forgive Zilu being "rough and rude" in the Master's opinion (11.18) because of his kindness and generosity (5.26)? Or perhaps his sensitivity to the meaning of the *Book of Poetry* (1.15)?

In this way readers may obtain insights into their own ordering of values and how they weigh the personality traits of others; key elements in personal understanding, which Confucius was always at pains to promote.

Similarly, in the course of participating in this kind of interactive engagement with the text readers will probably come to identify, at least to some extent, with one of the students more than the others, with the answers given to that student's questions by the Master taking on an added significance both as window and mirror. Consider, for example, the answer Confucius gives to Zigong when the latter inquires about *ren* in 15.10, keeping in mind that this student is an altogether social person, always inquiring about the Master's evaluation of others. Contrast this with the very different answer given to the same question when asked by the quieter, more introspective Yan Hui in 12.1; can we not obtain an insight into the nature of *ren* as Confucius employs the term from these differing responses?

In addition to the fifteen students mentioned a number of times, three others, seemingly of personal importance to Confucius are, rather surprisingly, mentioned only once or twice in the text, but bear noting here because of that importance. The first is his own son, Bo Yu, exhorted by his father in the two analects in which he appears (16.13 and 17.10) to intensify his study of the classical writings of poetry and rituals. The second, Bo Niu, was described by Confucius as excelling in his conduct (11.3), but even more important, when on his deathbed caused the Master to lose his composure in grief, an unprecedented happenstance save for the similar occasion where his favorite, Yan Hui, was also passing to his reward. (6.10 for Bo Niu, 11.9-11 for Yan Hui).

The third student that needs to be noted here is Zengxi, who appears only in 11.26. But this is a significant analect for a number of reasons, not least for what it says about the Master's abilities to delight in easygoing, altogether human activities as he can similarly delight in carrying out the most formal rituals of rank, protocol and other public business. Zengxi is a peer of Confucius, for his son Zengzi, or Master Zeng, is also a student, and one of the more renowned of them, establishing his own branch of the lineage begun by his teacher (and his father, who was perhaps less a student of Confucius than a like-minded colleague). 11.26 is a healthy antidote to anyone who would read the *Analects* as basically a completely outdated account of a stuffy, etiquette-bound martinet rather than a celebrator of life and its joys despite its sorrows who continues to have much to say of direct relevance to the world's peoples today.

To summarize these brief suggestions for readers to deepen their acquaintance with the text overall: after forming at least a tentative opinion of what kind of persons the students were after reading about each of them fully, with care and detail, the reader is then encouraged to reflect on the reasons for their opinion; why, in the end, do I (or do I not) find this person admirable, and to be emulated? After answering this question it might be well for the reader to then think about which one of the students he or she most nearly resembles, and then go back to re-read yet again and again the analects in which the kindred spirit appears; the text will, with effort, cease being solely a window through which the reader looks at the *dramatis personae* therein as it becomes a mirror of and for the reader engaged in conversation with them.

Finally, readers will have noted that I refer to the people mentioned in the *Analects* studying with Confucius as "students," rather than the much more common "disciples." Confucius did not have what we would today call a philosophy, certainly not a systematic philosophy; nor was he a prophet, and he didn't have or suggest a creed either. Thus he didn't have followers in the sense of discipleship, and in Sima Qian's quote about him having 77 persons as students, the referring term employed by Confucius is simply *ren* 人, "person." While the lineages that developed after his death all traced their teachings to him, they were somewhat different teachings, probably having relatively little in common except a focus on training for official position, and perhaps for their maintaining the Master's motivation and commitment to make their own students better persons. At the same time, as we can see from the discussion of 11.26 above, Zeng Xi was very probably less a "student" of the Master than a friend, or "associate." Thus, although I will continue to use the term "student" to refer to the lot of them, readers should understand it as shorthand for "students, friends and associates."

Chapter 7
THE MASTER

There are a few good biographies of Confucius in English, but just as it is better to become acquainted with his students directly from the text, so, too, with their teacher: the *Analects* contains a sufficient number of autobiographical and biographical statements about him to enable the careful reader to take a measure of the man when they feel it is important to do so. The measuring is not always easy, however, for the same reason that makes assessing the students a difficult task at times: a number of the relevant statements do not sit well with others equally relevant. The inflexibility he says he dislikes, for example, in 9.4 and 14.32 seems to be amply in evidence in much of Book 10 and elsewhere, when it comes to the niceties of ritual performance. And we must also wonder why, in at least some cases, he gives such divergent opinions of the same student.

With much of the evidence thus at least somewhat ambiguous, it is not surprising that differing views of who he was – and who he thought he was – have been held by a great many Chinese over the centuries, and by many in the West. But every contemporary reader would do well to form at least a tentative overall view of the man before turning to the work of his biographers. There is no doubt that he was a complex person, and consequently his words and actions can be weighed differently, and in differing proportions.

One important issue on which today's readers will have to weigh in on is the extent to which they believe Confucius would have condoned much of the authoritarianism that marred much familial and governmental life in later Chinese history. On the one hand, there are indeed many passages in the *Analects* suggesting the appropriateness of deference, obedience, and loyalty much of the time, especially with respect to fathers and rulers. But at other times he does not seem conservative in this respect at all.

See, for example, 2.24 or 14.22, in the text, or a key chapter (15) in the later *Chinese Classic of Family Reverence* -- which achieved canonical status – which reads as follows:

> ... Zengzi said: "I venture to ask whether children may be deemed filial simply by obeying every command of their father?" "What on earth are you saying?" Confucius responded . . . . "[I]f confronted by reprehensible behavior on his father's part, a son cannot but remonstrate with him, and if confronted by reprehensible behavior on the ruler's part, a minister has no choice but to remonstrate with the ruler. Hence remonstrance is the only response to inappropriate behavior. How could simply obeying the commands of one's father be deemed filial?"

We may, however, learn much of Confucius from the *Analects* itself; it has always been one of the main sources of our knowledge of Confucius, utilized by every one of his biographers since Sima Qian wrote the first one in the early Han Dynasty, as a part of his *magnum opus* the *Collected Records*. The only other early sources of information about the Master with any claim to reliability are a few statements in the *Mencius*, and in the *Zuo Commentary on the Spring and Autumn Annals*.

In brief, the accepted standard account of his life is that he was born in the state of Song, moving to the nearby state of Lu when he was a youngster. We might speculate that a part of the reason he centered his thinking on the family and family reverence *(xiao)* later in life was because his own was so bleak. Confucius was supposedly a distant descendant of the Shang royal house deposed by the Zhou in ca. 1050 BCE. The Shang survivors of the Zhou conquest were said to have been given a sinecure in Lu, hence his affection for his homeland. (But he never claimed an aristocratic pedigree.)

If the legends are to be believed, Confucius had 9 half-sisters and a handicapped or deformed half-brother before he was born to his sire's third mate when the former was 60. The father died three years later, and the boy's mother died when he was 17. His name as a young man, Zhong Ni, is made up of two graphs, the first meaning the "middle son," and the second is the name of the mountain where he was supposedly born, Mt. Ni *(Nishan)*. While pregnant, his mother had gone to the mountain to pray for a healthy son, and according to later mythology the boy was born in a cave near the bottom of the mountain (more nearly a tall hill), with a dragon making an appearance to inform the new mother that her offspring would become an "Uncrowned King."

(The area of Nishan is now the home of a new Confucian academy, hotel and conference center.)

Although supposedly his father had been a military officer, the family was relatively poor throughout Confucius's childhood, as he himself attests in 9.6. If he had teachers we don't know who they were, or what he did until early middle age, except that he seems to have done some teaching. After serving in relatively minor posts in Lu he incurred the wrath of his superiors and was discharged and sent into exile (according to some accounts, and the recent movie *Confucius*). Whereas in other accounts he resigned and voluntarily left the state with some of his students and wandered in several neighboring states for almost 13 years, altogether unsuccessful in securing official employment in any of them. (That he resigned instead of being exiled is also the account portrayed in the lovely new ballet about his life with the same name.)

After enduring several hardships (and good times, too, in all probability), he returned to his homeland, and continued teaching until his death in 479 BCE at the age of 73. Of his own family we know very little indeed. From 5.3 we learn that he had a daughter, and at least one son, Bo Yu, mentioned twice in 16.13 and 17.10. The text makes no mention, however, of the Master's wife, or wives, if he had more than one, or concubines, if he had any at all.

The hagiographies began about 500 years after his death, bearing scant affinities with any historical facts. One legend is, however, of significance in my view, for the glimpses it gives us both of how Confucius was perceived, and children depicted. The story goes that one day, while riding in his carriage, the Master passed by a young boy of 7, Xiang Tuo, building houses in the sand and mud, oblivious to the carriage. Confucius dismounted, the legend continues, and began interrogating the boy on a number of matters, with the boy, always very polite, giving the correct answer to all of them. Then the boy, equally politely, began to interrogate his interrogator in turn, and soon stumped him, after which Confucius asked the boy to be his teacher. What stands out in this tale, to me at least, is that the boy is not only an exemplary model of intelligence for other children, but a model of deportment as well, always properly deferential to his elders. And Confucius is no less exemplary for his capacity to admit error, and to be anxious to learn from anyone at all who might have something to teach him, as the *Analects* also frequently attests.

After becoming acquainted with the Confucius found in the *Analects,* readers may well want to dip into the biographies of him briefly described in the bibliography at the end of this book.

Chapter 8
ON KNOWING

The most basic reason for reading a book, apart from the pure pleasure thereof, is to gain *knowledge* of some kind or another, and it is therefore fitting that when we think of how best to approach the *Analects* we examine the concept of "knowledge" as it is reflected and embodied in the text itself.

Translators have used a variety of English words for each of the key philosophical and religious terms in the *Analects,* as the Concordance of Key Terms (Appendix II) makes clear. One term that has not been taken to be multivocal, however, is *zhi* 知, which has almost invariably been translated by others as "knowledge" or "wisdom" nominally, and verbally as "to know." It is surely linked to commendable human qualities for Confucius, and indeed it is the philosophically significant most frequently occurring term in the *Analects:* It appears 118 times – i.e., more often than *ren* 仁 109 or *junzi* 君子 108 -- a third more frequently than *dao* 道 90, half again as frequently as *li* 禮 75, and it occurs six times more often than *xiao* 孝 19. A major reason for the relative neglect of attention to *zhi* when studying the *Analects* is that if it is rendered simply as "knowledge," it appears philosophically unproblematic, unlike the other graphs in the early Confucian ethical lexicon, onto which no single English term can be easily mapped. But it is important to understand why *zhi* is no less multivocal than the other key philosophical and religious terms, for much of both the form and content of the brief discussions between Confucius and his students that comprise the *Analects* can be easily misconstrued if the complex connotations of *zhi* are not properly contextualized..

While English "knowledge" has several shades of meaning, and has meant different things to different Western philosophers, it most commonly means "knowing that," in the sense of awareness of facts about the way the world is: "Water freezes at 32 degrees Fahrenheit," "Reptiles are cold-blooded," "Mercury is the planet closest to our sun," and so forth. This is the most common form of knowledge as we tend to think of it today, and teachers regularly test whether or not students have this knowledge by giving them True/False or multiple-choice examinations.

A similar type of "knowing that" has to do with explanations of facts, i.e., knowledge of scientific laws or theories, from Boyle's Law to Darwinian Evolution or General Relativity Theory. In these cases we can test knowledge either employing mathematical formulae or essay examinations. Relatedly, one more pattern of "knowing that" is when a poem, speech, or other significant element of prior speech/writing has been memorized, as "Tommy knows the Gettysburg Address by heart."

Aside from occasional brief comments about the significance of studying the *Book of Odes* and *Book of History* carefully, these three closely linked kinds of knowledge are seldom found in the *Analects*. Rather should Confucius be read as modeling behavior – including verbal behavior – and encouraging and teaching his students to always act appropriately, and to develop appropriate attitudes toward those appropriate actions, which together make up most usages of *zhi* in the text.

Clearly no mere written examination could thus test *zhi*, and an oral "test" would not be evaluated strictly on the basis of what the student actually said – even if reciting an ode from the *Book of Odes*-- but also on his tone of voice in saying it, his demeanor overall, and equally, his past and present behaviors. If so, "knowledge," is not the most perspicacious translation of *zhi* most of the time. Confucius is not so much describing the world for his students as he is giving them guidance on how best to live in it.

Consider passages in the text which do not square at all well with translating *zhi* as "knowledge" in the sense of knowing facts or theories, or rote memorization.

In 7.20, Confucius says:

> "I am not the kind of person who has had *zhi* from birth. Rather, loving antiquity, I am earnest in seeking it out.

And relatedly, in 16.9: *zhi* had from birth is the highest; *zhi* obtained through learning is next highest.

Even though most translators have rendered these occurrences of *zhi* as "knowledge," surely not even a thoroughgoing rationalist would claim that we are born with facts and theories in our heads, even in rudimentary form.

From these and related usages of *zhi* in the *Analects*, especially in its more philosophically and spiritually important occurrences, it is perhaps best defined as *a sense of what it is most fitting to do in our interactions with our fellow human beings, understanding why, performing those actions, and achieving a sense of well-being from so doing.* This is obviously far too cumbersome a locution to employ in translation, and it is not possible to merely gloss the term and thereafter simply transliterate it, because {*zhi*} is a very common phoneme in Chinese; eighteen different graphs having little or nothing to do with each other semantically are all transliterated as *zhi* in the *Analects* alone. Moreover, there are indeed some passages in which "knowledge," "certainty," or "understanding" does indeed render *zhi* better than any other English term. But in the great majority of cases, a better word for most occasions of the "knowing" *zhi* in the *Analects* is "realize," which my collaborator Roger Ames first proposed in his *Thinking Through Confucius*. It is epistemically as strong in English as "know" with respect to truth conditions, for just as I cannot *know* that today is Tuesday if it is in fact Thursday, I can't *realize* it either. That is to say, if I may be said to know or realize X, X must be the case (unlike when x follows dispositional terms like "hope," "think," "believe," etc.).

"Realize" is also an appropriate term for *zhi* most of the time because of another way the English language functions. If "finalize" is "to make final," and "personalize" is "to make personal," then "realize" can mean "to make real" in just the sense intended in the *Analects*; that is, "to put into practice." For Confucius, persons who don't practice what they preach aren't really preaching anything worth listening to, and surely are not worthy of our audience. *Tu quoque* arguments have a force in Chinese thought – and at least occasionally in Western thought as well, as the "Cast the first stone" statement of Jesus shows – but are technically condemned as fallacious in matters of formal logic. It is not that the Chinese are in any way illogical, but rather that they place as much emphasis on authenticity in their rhetoric as they do on what we would consider pure rationality; in Book I of the *Analects* alone the exhortation to "make good on one's word" is the theme of six of the sixteen sections.

A few examples of the naturalness of "realize" for *zhi*:

> Children must realize (*zhi*) the age of their parents. On the one hand it is a source of joy, on the other, of fear. (4.21)
> " I [Confucius] am so eager to teach and learn that I forget to eat, enjoy myself so much I forget to worry, and do not even realize (*zhi*) that old age is nearing."(7.19)
>
> "At fifty, I realized (*zhi*) the propensities of *tian*.)" (*tian ming*天命) (2.4)

To make real, however, to put into practice, is not enough; we must have the proper stance and feelings toward what we are making real in our conduct. Consider a passage that deals with *xiao*, familial reverence, one of the highest excellences for the early Confucians (2.8):

> The Master said: "*xiao* lies in showing the proper countenance. As for the young contributing their energies when there is work to be done, and deferring to their elders when there is wine and food to be had – how can merely doing these things be considered *xiao*? "(2.8).

The point of these and similar passages is that we must not only be aware of our responsibilities, we must understand how best to discharge them with respect to what is most appropriate in the circumstances, perform the actions in a ritually proper manner as well (the *li*), and we must have the correct attitude toward performing these actions. Together, this is how *zhi* is exhibited.

But how to convey *zhi* ?

First, we must keep uppermost in mind that language use is *a social practice*. We are inclined to focus on the informative uses of language, that is, the transmission of *knowledge that*. But I believe readers will profit more from the *Analects* if *zhi* as "realize" is understood as more closely akin to *knowing how* , *knowing about, or knowing to;* most of the Master's use of language is best appreciated if, following Chad Hansen, we see it as praxis-guiding verbal behavior. On this interpretation, most of what the Master says to his students should be read as imperatives, despite the declarative syntactic structure that must be imposed on many of his "sentences" when they are rendered into English. Or put another way, Confucius should be construed fairly uniformly as not so much concerned to have his students absorb information -- which he could do merely by stating the information – as he is to have his students act and/or react, or at least be disposed to act and/or react, in specific ways; for the success of which he may have to perform a variety of different speech acts, depending on the circumstances, and the background and readiness for instruction on the part of his individual student listener(s).

What may be surprising to some people is that scholars of the Chinese sciences can also read *zhi* pretty much as I am suggesting here; the connotations of the term are not confined to what may be taken as the aesthetic, ethical and religious dimensions of our lives. Or perhaps better stated, the aesthetic, ethical and religious dimensions of our lives are what make our lives truly human lives. Nathan Sivin, for example, who has made detailed studies of Chinese medical, astronomical, alchemical, mathematical and other sciences, has said:

> *Chih* [*zhi*] refers to understanding and recognition of significance as aspects of knowledge, not to objective factual knowledge isolated from the act of understanding and evaluating.

Evidence for this reading of *zhi* abounds in the text of the

Analects and is straightforward: many Western readers are confused when they read Confucius giving different answers to the same question in different passages, failing to appreciate that the questioner is a different person in each case, as we found in Chapter 6, with the key passage (11.22) important enough to bear repeating here:

> Zilu inquired, "On learning something, should one act upon it?" The Master said, "While your father and elder brothers are still alive, how could you, on learning something, act upon it?"
>
> Then Ranyou asked the same question. The Master replied, "On learning something, act on it." Gongxi Hua said, "When Zilu asked the question, you observed that his father and elder brothers are still alive, but when Ranyou asked the same question you told him to act on what he learns. I am confused – could you explain this to me?"
>
> The Master replied, "Ranyou is diffident, and so I urged him on. But Zilu has the energy of two, and so I sought to rein him in."

Perfect examples of "praxis-guiding" discourse for the students.

A final comment on *zhi*: I want to suggest that throughout the text, the Master's urging us to "make real" his teachings are, in the end, to be construed not simply as ethical, psychological, social and political advice – although they are importantly all of these, too – but more basically as religious or *spiritual* instructions for how to live a meaningful life. We will take up this theme in more detail jointly with some others in the following four chapters.

Chapter 9
READING THE TEXT: IS WHAT IT SAYS TRUE?

In the last chapter I suggested that a basic function of language as it was employed by Confucius in conversations with his students in the *Analects* was as "praxis-guiding discourse." That is to say, he was not so much concerned to convey factual information, or propound a theory, as he was to have his students respond in a particular way to the topic on which he was discoursing or had been asked about. By putting ourselves into the text we can better understand the remark of Zhu Xi quoted in Chapter 2, that when reading, "It is like talking [with the sages] face to face." Here I want to elaborate on that theme somewhat because of its importance in interacting with the text of the *Analects*.

A major implication of this analysis of the Master's use of language, and the function and meaning of *zhi* as "realize" is that contemporary readers should resist asking of any specific statement of the Master's, "Is it true?" Only when language is used in declarative sentences to state facts in the indicative mood should the predicate verb phrase "is true" (or "is false"), as used in both philosophical and vernacular English, be applied to them. But a great many of the statements of Confucius and his students in the *Analects* should not to be read as declarative sentences despite having that syntactic form in English, but rather as imperatives, or at least as strong behavioral suggestions. When he says in 13.18, to take a famous example, that in his village "A father covers for his son, and a son covers for his father" he is not making an anthropological statement as participant-observer; we clearly understand him to be telling us that in any conflict between family and state, the family must always win.

Put another way, if speakers of a language see its primary function as praxis-guiding discourse, then a specific term/graph for "truth" or "is true" applicable to declarative sentences stating facts will not be an important lexical item in the language, and indeed, early Chinese has no such term in its lexicon. (Nor, for that matter, is there a close analogue for the English "fact"). "True" is at times found in English translations of the *Analects*, including our A&R, but in the sense of "true friend" or "true North." i.e. being authentic, genuine, upright, or simply real; not as a property of declarative statements which state facts.

To note what might seem to be a semantic oddity, however, is not in any way to suggest that there was some conceptual weakness or naiveté on the part of early Chinese thinkers in general or Confucius in particular. If one's culture employs language primarily as a vehicle for conveying straightforward information, it had better have a term for distinguishing the accurate from the inaccurate information conveyed, which "true" and "false" do very well. But if a more significant function of human language in another culture is as praxis-guiding discourse, then the evaluative terms needed will more nearly approximate "appropriate" and "inappropriate" than "true" and "false." – and the former (*yi* 義 and *bu yi* 不義) are central terms in the Confucian ethical lexicon, as we noted in Chapter 5.

It is worth noting in this regard that "appropriate" is also the correct term to employ in describing many English speech acts as well. "A watched pot never boils," for example, is certainly not true (unless the stove is turned off), but is surely *appropriate* to say at times – even when the listener is not observing cookware – as are other little homilies like "An apple a day keeps the doctor away." Depending on the person we're addressing, and when, we also make inconsistent generalizations at times which cannot simultaneously be true, but may well be appropriate to say to particular persons in specific circumstances. "You can't teach an old dog new tricks," and "you're never too old to learn" are one such pairing, and "Act in haste, repent at leisure," and "He who hesitates is lost" is another.

My own favorite example of the necessity to frequently ask *why* a person said something as opposed to *what*, exactly, was said, is taken from an article by the noted physicist Robert Oppenheimer, who wrote:

> If we ask whether the electron's position changes with time, we must say "No." If we ask whether the position of the electron remains the same, we must say "No." If we ask whether the

> electron is at rest, we must say "No." If we ask
> whether it is in motion, we must say "No."

These statements are of course incredible. It is very difficult for any of us to accept them as literal fact, for they violate very basic principles of logic and ordinary physics, and they contradict a lifetime of the testimony of our senses about the physical world.

But if read less literally, it should not be difficult for us to believe there is a "truth" in what Oppenheimer said, just as for Confucius. We must read those highly unusual sentences of Oppenheimer's indirectly, for clearly he is using them to help us gain a little purchase on some highly unusual features of the world of quantum mechanics as developed by modern physicists; at the least, he is issuing a clear warning that we should not think of quanta as very, very, *very* small bits of matter.

There are a number of other implications of this analysis of "truth," the most significant of which, I would suggest, is that the Master's urging us to "make real" his teachings should, in the end, be construed as instructions for personal cultivation that frequently have a spiritual dimension for how to live a meaningful life in a seemingly random world not of our own making, being able to go through the affairs of life without "being perplexed," as *Analects* 9.29 and 14.28 tell us.

This point requires some elaboration. For the most part, we have little difficulty describing our perceptions, what we perceive with our senses: "There are three oak trees in front of that house;" "That sounds like Mozart's 'Jupiter' Symphony;" "The soup has a lot of salt in it," etc. That is to say, what we see, hear, taste, smell and touch can usually be described clearly and accurately in ordinary language, English or otherwise. And here again questions of truth and falsity are appropriately raised: "Those are elms, not oaks;" "You're right, that is the 'Jupiter;'" "Sorry, I misread one Tsp. to be one Tbs."

Our *experiences,* however, are often much harder to communicate easily; things and events that move us deeply we frequently find difficult to describe. Some of these experiences may legitimately be seen as religious experiences, as when Wittgenstein referred to them as "The sense of being absolutely safe." We can read that line, and say, truthfully, "Wittgenstein described religious experience as 'the sense of being absolutely safe.'" But what is it like to *experience* being absolutely safe? Blending sacred with secular experience, we may surely believe John Donne was altogether sincere when he said that "Any man's death diminishes me, for I am involved in mankind," but what might the feeling of diminution be like? Solely in the secular, what is it like to "live deliberately," as Thoreau explained he wanted to do when he moved from Concord to Walden Pond for two years?

The relevance of the distinction between perception and experience to the *Analects* lies in a parallel distinction between conduct and motivation. It is common in Western moral thinking that one must meet one's obligations whether they are pleasant or distasteful. And one is moral if they are met, and if not, not. For Confucius, however (as well as for most of his successors), in addition to meeting your responsibilities, you must discipline yourself to have a proper attitude toward them, you must come to *want* to fulfill those responsibilities in order to lead a maximally fulfilling life in concert with others. But how best to inculcate that sense, that feeling, that desire?   Consider 2.7:

> [The Master said] "Those today who are filial are considered so because they are able to provide for their parents. But even dogs and horses are given that much care. If you do not revere your parents, what is the difference?"

On another occasion Confucius remarked autobiographically (7.34) that

> " . . [W]hat may be said about me is simply that I continue my studies without respite and instruct others without growing weary."

To which the student Gongxi Hua replied,

> "It is precisely this commitment that we students are unable to learn."

In sum, it is best to see Confucius as not only concerned to conduct himself appropriately at all times, but teaching (speaking) appropriately as well, for he is consistently endeavoring to get his students not only to "do the right thing, " but equally to instill a proper attitude toward their actions (and the actions of others). Thus, if the concept of "truth" in anything like its contemporary English usages is applicable to understanding Confucius, perhaps, like his ancient Hebrew brethren, it can be said that he believed living in it was superior to speaking it, with both having to be done appropriately at all times.

Chapter 10
ROLES, FAMILIES, AND SOCIETY

Because Confucius is concerned to describe, analyze and evaluate human conduct, we are inclined to view him as an ethicist. And in some respects he is indeed an ethicist, but it would be a mistake to impose too much of the conceptual framework of Western moral philosophy on the *Analects* if we are going to maximize what may be learned from it about ethics. Here I do not merely mean we should avoid imposing the contemporary concept-cluster surrounding "morals" on the text as discussed in Chapter 5, but also that we should not expect to find an ethical *theory* there. At the end of the day, Confucius is probably best understood as concerned to make us better persons; he has a general vision, but not what we would today consider a philosophical theory – of ethics or anything else.

For Confucius, the roots of ethical conduct are grounded in the family, and he focuses on the responsibilities of family members as determined by their role(s) in family life: father, mother, son, daughter; grandmothers and grandfathers; brothers and sisters, aunts and uncles. Because everyone is thus related closely to others from birth, the idea of human beings as free, autonomous (and rational) individuals would not have occurred to Confucius, for in the actual world in which everyone lives when not philosophizing we are always encumbered by our responsibilities. We therefore cannot be autonomous individuals

— in the usual sense of being lawgivers unto ourselves -- for that concept presupposes that there are actions we take that have no impact on anyone else, and against the background of Confucian relationality there are no such actions. ("Freedom" is also a term for which there is no close lexical equivalent in classical Chinese.)

This suggests that a very basic question of ethics will be how best to properly meet the responsibilities that encumber us all, *and* come to enjoy meeting them. Put another way, what is the proper way for a son to conduct himself, what feelings should he develop toward those affected by his conduct, and toward his conduct itself? Seen in this light, it might be best to approach Confucius initially as concerned ethically with the *roles* that people occupy, for much of the *Analects* is devoted to discussions of them: how to be a good child; the responsibilities of parents and elders toward the young; the loyalty ministers owe their ruler; the responsibility of the ruler to see to the well-being of the people; what it is to be a friend; and more.

This is not to say that Confucius was not sensitive to *individuality*, for the *Analects* shows throughout that he knew that, and how, each of the students were unique persons; indeed, his pedagogic strategy depended on that knowledge. Rather is it the concept of unique persons as free, autonomous individuals that we probably should not impose on the Master when considering his ethical views.

Another reason that it is highly problematic to impose a

Western moral framework on the text is that it tempts us to look for moral principles that we will expect to be embedded there, and will therefore be disappointed when we can find very few, the so-called negative Golden Rule found in 12.2 and 15.24 being the example most often put forward. Rather than a concern to find moral principles that should be binding on everyone, i.e., universal, Confucius seemed much more attentive to the *particular*, in the sense of being context-specific and person specific, stemming from everyday human experience.

Again, appreciating his orientation toward the family as the basic locus from which people develop as ethical human beings can help us understand his particularism. Clearly what persons should do in a situation at home will depend on which other members of the family they are engaged with, and at what time: the way I should acknowledge and repay a kindness from my grandmother will almost surely not be the same as it would be if the recipient of my attentions were my father, younger sister, or uncle. It is largely for this reason that "appropriate" seems a better translation for *yi* than "right" or "moral;" what is an appropriate response to my grandmother in a specific situation will almost certainly not be the same if it is my little sister to whom I will be responding. And even if it is only the interactions with my grandmother that are under consideration, clearly what is appropriate for me to do may well be different when I am 22 than when I was 8.

The ethics of Confucius is not confined to the family, of

course, although it serves as the training ground for the other roles people will live in the larger community, and state. The role of friend is a bridge from the family to the outside world. Learning how to properly interact with our own grandparents is the best preparation for learning how to properly interact with other grandparents, and indeed with all elders. The way we engage with younger family members is a model for engaging with all who are younger than ourselves. Further, specific family relationships serve as the model for other relationships similarly constituted, but with non-kin. The father-son, relationship, for example, sets the pattern not only for uncle-nephew interactions also within the family, but for teacher-student, master-apprentice, and ruler-minister beyond the home as well.

Much textual evidence also suggests that Confucius envisioned the state as a family writ large, with the ruler as the father and mother of his subjects, responsible for their well-being at all times. Like any parent, the ruler must see to the welfare of his "children," who reciprocally owe loyalty to him. These and other mutual responsibilities attendant on roles are hierarchical throughout, but not elitist because the roles can be generalized as holding between benefactors and beneficiaries, and for Confucius, everyone occupies both positions fairly regularly throughout their lives, sometimes with the same person: I was beneficiary of my parents when I was young, becoming their benefactor as they became aged and infirm; I am benefactor to my friend when she needs my help, beneficiary when I need hers.

In contemporary Western culture, especially in the U.S., "family values" are closely linked with very conservative views, most of them also linked with one form of religious fundamentalism or another. But today's reader of the *Analects* should resist imposing *that* view of the family on Confucius too quickly, for a progressive ordering of values may also stem from his particularist ethics grounded in the family and focusing on roles. And because families are going to continue to dominate human life as far into the future (who else would raise the young?), re-configuring family values with an eye to family lineages is an intellectual task everyone might profit from entertaining.

One objection that is always and quickly raised against any particularistic ethics that does not employ principles is to ask where one gets guidelines for ascertaining what the "appropriate" thing to do might be in times of conflict. For example, the *Analects* makes clear that if called upon to serve in government Confucius believes we should do so. But suppose that after some time on the job we conclude the ruler is not a good man, not a *real* ruler; he is corrupt, pleasure-seeking, and unconcerned about the welfare of his subjects. What are we to do?

The reader looking for a general criterion or abstract principle to help answer this question will, I think, search in vain. But that does not mean Confucius has no advice for us. Keeping in mind that Confucius works from concrete experience, he will tell us we must first ask of *this* ruler, the one we know and serve, is he reformable? If, upon considered reflection we answer the question affirmatively, we must then ask whether we think *we* have the requisite skills, abilities and temperament to reform him. If self-reflection yields another affirmative answer, we continue to serve the ruler, taking as our model the exemplar King Wen (19.22), titular founder of the Zhou Dynasty, who was most famous for being a loyal vassal of the last Shang Dynasty Emperor, remonstrating with him to cease his evil ways and become a true ruler. If the answer to the first question is "yes," -- the ruler is reformable – but "no" to the second – we don't believe we ourselves can do the reforming – then Confucius himself becomes our model, supposedly retiring from government when he couldn't reform it (2.21).

Finally, if we conclude, with respect to the first question, that the ruler we are serving is *not* reformable, we have a third model to follow: that of King Wu, son of King Wen, who was the actual founder of the Zhou Dynasty because he raised the flag of rebellion and overthrew the evil last Emperor of the Shang (19.22 again). Thus there is always a way to answer the question of what is appropriate conduct for us in any given situation, but it will seldom if ever be a *general* answer. The question of what to do with an abusive father mirrors that of the bad ruler: who could possibly tell better how to handle the situation (do what is appropriate) than the people who know the father the most intimately?

Families always have been the center of Chinese life, and for the most part remain such. One major reason for their strength has been that our responsibilities to the other members of our families have never been confined to caring for those now living, for we also have major responsibilities to and for the dead, to a sketch of which we must now turn.

Chapter 11
ANCESTOR VENERATION

Archaeological work in China reveals funerary and burial practices honoring the dead that go back to the early Neolithic period. When ancestor veneration began is not known, but it was well established by the time of the Shang Dynasty (traditional dates 1766-1052 BCE) – i.e., a millennium before the time of Confucius.

During that time it was believed that gods brought blessings or curses on the living, but unfortunately the living could not communicate directly with the gods in supplication or prayer, but had to ask their ancestors to serve as intermediaries, interceding with the deities on behalf of their descendants. Even in the Master's own time, and later yet, the ancestors were thought to be able to bring good or bad fortune to the living, depending on how well or poorly the rituals commemorating them were conducted. (And powerful families must have powerful ancestors, so one might be tempted to offer sacrifices to them even if they are not from one's own line, which explains the general rebuke Confucius gives in 2.24: "Sacrificing to ancestral spirits other than one's own is being unctuous.")

Families in a descent line would twice annually gather to sacrifice to the spirit of their patriarch (and often matriarch), both of which were performed with great solemnity, followed by a festival gathering in kin solidarity. In the *Analects* Confucius regularly quotes from *The Book of Odes,* which has several accounts of such rituals in verse. One is given here, and the contemporary reader of the *Analects* should attempt to retain the picture conjured up in this ode (translated by James Legge) whenever the text makes reference to honoring ancestors:

> Very hard have we striven that the rites might be without mistake. The skillful recitant conveys the message, goes and gives it to the personator:
>
> "Fragrant were your pious offerings, the spirits enjoyed their drink and food. They assign to you a hundred blessings. According to their hopes, their rules, all was orderly and swift, all was straight and sure. Forever they will bestow upon you good Store; myriads and tens of myriads."
>
> The rites have all been accomplished, The bells and the drums are ready.
>
> The personator ascends the seat and the skillful recitant conveys the message:
>
> "The Spirits are all drunk."
> The august 'Dead One' [personator] then rises
> And is seen off with drums and bells;
> The Spirits and Protectors have gone home.
> Then the stewards and our lord's lady
> Clear away the dishes with all speed,
> While the uncles and brothers
> All go off to the lay feast.
>
> The musicians go in and play,
> That after-blessings may be secured.

> Your viands are passed round;
> No one is discontented, all are happy;
> ...."The Spirits," they say, "enjoyed their
> drink and food...."

There are several noteworthy elements in this ode. First, the ceremony is highly ritualized. (More on this in the following chapter). Second, it is celebratory. The clan has gathered for a communal ancestral sacrifice, in this case marking the anniversary of the patriarchal ancestor's death. Everything has gone well, everyone is satisfied, and the attendant good feelings are aesthetic and social no less than familial and religious. These ancestral observances are at the heart of Confucian perspectives on the *li* (ritual) and consequently are central to early Confucian spirituality.

Readers of this and similar odes, as well as the *Analects*, must bear in mind that Chinese persons are identified and understood significantly as they stand in relation to and with other persons, dead no less than living. That is to say, for the Master I am not seen fundamentally as an autonomous individual, but rather first and foremost as a son, grandson and great-grandson; then a father, then a father-in-law and grandfather; also a husband, a teacher, a student, a colleague, a neighbor, and more. When all of these roles have been specified, and their interrelations made clear, then for Confucius I have been fairly well uniquely identified as a person; he will know who I am. I will have a place and a role at the ancestral sacrifice, in relation to others who will have similarly related roles and places.

At least one of the roles that everyone participating in this *li* sacrificial ritual bears is that of descendant. A peculiar part of this ritual (peculiar at first blush, at any rate), is that of the personator, the Chinese graph for which is exactly the same as that for "corpse." (*shi* 尸). A young person – usually a grandson or granddaughter of the deceased – literally "sits in" for him or her in the place of honor. They have earlier gone through purification rituals to prepare themselves for their ceremonial role. They are fed much food and drink during the ritual, and are regularly asked to bestow blessings on all the descendants gathered together offering the sacrifices (which they seem to do most of the time if the rituals are being performed correctly).

Such a ritual certainly lessens the distance between the living and the dead. The ancestor being venerated at the sacrifice is literally eating and drinking the offerings made to him or her, and also *talking*, via the personator, to the participants in the ritual sacrifice. Why is the ancestor venerated so? Because, as we identify ourselves not only with our immediate families intergenerationally, we can come to identify also with those who came several generations before us – which, for the Confucians as I read them, I would call a spiritual exercise. And if we indeed come to feel a part of the family of our ancestral lines, then clearly we owe a deep debt of gratitude to those who preceded us and have given rise to the descendant families of which we are a part, and of which they remain a part as well; psychoculturally they remain present.

Something else to note about the ode is its intergenerationality. Descendants of the deceased will be many, and of greatly varying ages. And just as we keep our links with the past through participating in the time-honored rituals, by having the young as fellow participants we are preparing future generations to learn the rituals, perform them, and carry them on in turn, modifying them as needed by changing circumstances, but remaining linked. So it is not just a feeling of kinship with our fellow human beings alive when we are – i.e., our parents and children -- that Confucian rituals are designed to induce, but, at the higher levels, a feeling of kinship with others who have preceded us, and those who will follow; a bond, in other words, of oneself and others. Against this background, we may interpret a well-known passage from the *Analects*:

> The disciple Zilu said, "We would like to hear what it isthat you, Master, would like most to do." The Master replied, "I would like to bring peace and contentment to the aged, share relationships of trust and fellow-feeling with friends, and love and protect the young." (5.26)

At first reading this seems to be simply an autobiographical statement from a rather nice old man, but it is better, I believe, to see it as religious instructions for self-cultivation, linked closely to meeting one's responsibility to honor the ancestors, and derive satisfaction and pleasure from so doing, all through participation in *li*.

In sum, ancestor veneration has so thoroughly permeated all dimensions of Chinese society since before the time of Confucius that it is difficult to imagine what the culture would be like without it. Widely practiced many centuries before him, he provided different but no less spiritual grounds for maintaining the rich ritual tradition that cemented family life that has endured ever since – including today, even though under threat.

Chapter 12

RITUALS (THE *LI*) AND SPIRITUAL CULTIVATION

Just as ancestor veneration cannot be practiced without ritual – the *li* -- Confucius cannot be understood without appreciating the importance he attached to the concept. It is one of the more frequently occurring philosophical terms in the *Analects*, and the reader will see in the Concordance (Appendix II) that more English words have and can be employed to translate it than for any other Chinese character on the list. Written 禮, the left side of the graph is a stylized representation signifying "to display," "to offer up," and hence came to be associated with the spirits, while the right side means something like "plenty," or "bountiful;" in it most ancient forms the graph appears to be either an altar with stones or jade tablets on it or in it; another interpretation of some archaic forms of the graph suggest vegetables sticking out of a sacrificial bowl mounted on a ritual tripod. Combined, "spirits coming to receive the sacrifice" might best approximate its original meaning.

The A&R translation of the text uses "ritual propriety" most frequently for *li*, but the reader will do well to try to keep at least some of the other English lexical possibilities in mind as well when coming across *li:* "rites," "etiquette," "ceremonies," "customs," " worship," "manners," and "sacramental," as well as "rituals," for *li* does appear to have most of these meanings on nearly every occasion of its use.

The concept of *li* might initially be difficult for today's reader of the *Analects* to take anywhere near as seriously as Confucius certainly did. First, we are inclined to distinguish between the customary rules of behavior (shaking hands), rules of etiquette (handwritten thank-you notes), manners (say "please"); rules of protocol (never touch the Queen), moral rules (you must never lie), and religious rules (daylight fasting during Ramadan), whereas all these kinds of rules seem to run together on a continuum as the concept of *li* functions in the *Analects*. Consequently the several connotations of the term must be kept in mind in coming to an understanding of its overarching significance for Confucius. In modern Western thought we would have to describe that significance as having aesthetic, ethical, social, political and religious dimensions. But it is not at all clear that Confucius would distinguish our behaviors in that way, for he saw the *li* as investing much of human life and most human activity, and doing so in an integrative manner.

The most important rituals were concentrated in court and family life. The latter are the most important for our understanding, because many of the court's rituals were the same as those of the family: centered in ancestor veneration, as we have already seen from reading the *Shijing* ode in the last chapter, where the *li* are the glue for family relations, and flowing out from there, are extended to the clan, to the community, to the kingdom, ultimately to "All Under Heaven' (*tian xia*, the world). For Confucius the *li* are the means of regulating the social and political intercourse of the Chinese peoples. At a more personal level, the *li* are necessary for children to express their respect and affection for parents; needed for the self-discipline that is a key component of personal cultivation; they are the essential link between our past, present and future; and because of all of these, they play a major role in assisting the follower of them to define the meaning of their lives by investing the *li* with meaning.

When reading the *Shijing* sacrificial ode for the first time, we may want to ask – almost cannot help but asking – did the early Chinese of the ode really believe the ancestor's spirit was partaking of the food and drink, was really talking through the medium of the personator? Is this the way they thought of being linked to the past? Or asked more relevantly with respect to the *Analects:* Did Confucius believe in the ghosts and spirits mentioned several times in the book?

Confucius provides a summary non-answer answer to this question in commenting on the importance of personally participating in the sacrifice as a gloss on an older statement, "Sacrifice to the spirits as if they were present." (3.12). This most succinct of statements illustrates well several key Confucian views.

First, there are ritual sacrifices that each of us is responsible for performing. Second, we must do the performing ourselves (i.e., not send the florist to lay the flowers on our mother's grave on the anniversary of her death). Third, and most important, Confucius was more attuned to and interested in what we would call psychological rather than metaphysical issues.

The best way to appreciate the significance of this last point is to take a few short passages from the accounts of purification rituals found in the *Li Ji* or *Records of Ritual* while harking back to the officiants at the ancestral sacrifice described in the ode quoted from the *Book of Odes:*

> The severest vigil and purification is maintained and carried on inwardly; a looser vigil is maintained externally. During such vigil mourners think of the departed, how and where they sat, how they smiled and spoke, what were their aims and views, what they delighted in, and what things they desired and enjoyed. *On the third day of such exercise the mourners will see those for whom it is employed.*
>
> On the day of sacrifice, when he enters the apartment (of the temple) *he will seem to see the deceased in place where their spirit-tablet is.* After he had moved about and performed his operations and is leaving at the door, he will seem to be arrested by hearing the sound of his movements, and will sigh as he seems to hear the sound of his sighing.
>
> Thus the family reverence taught by the ancient kings required that the eyes of the son should not forget the looks of his parents, nor his ears their voices; and that he should retain the memory of their aims, likings and wishes. As he gave full play to his love, *they seemed to live again*; and to his reverence, they *seemed to stand out before him.* . . . . [all italics added].

Against this background the question of the existence of ghosts and spirits *qua* ghosts and spirits is beside the point for understanding what Confucius was about. There is no tradition that has him editing the *Records of Ritual along* with others of the classics, but parts of that book do come from his time, and he may well have read these or similar passages; perhaps he even wrote them, as they clearly explain and elaborate on the importance of sacrificing to the ghosts and spirits "as if they were present." Confucius is never dismissive of the concept of "ghosts and spirits;" indeed, he says that if we are wise we will "respect" them -- but we will also "keep them at a distance" (6.22). Skeptics may want to dismiss these purification passages as hallucinatory, but it will probably be better for today's reader to think of going to a cemetery to pay respects to a departed family member or friend buried there, and "speaking" to the deceased at the gravesite. Why is that done?

These passages from the *Records of Ritual* should also be kept in mind when reading Book 10 of the *Analects*. At first blush the passages in it certainly appear to portray the Master as a world-class martinet, a stickler for detail that if followed, would seem not only to stifle any type of creativity or spontaneity, but also make it all but impossible simply to relax. Yet many passages in the text -- 11.26 paramount among them – show that Confucius was not a stuffed shirt, which suggests that in conjunction with remembering the purification passages, Book 10 should be read a number of times and reflected upon. Once more Zhu Xi proffers good advice to us:

> Read each passage over and over again until you are thoroughly familiar with it. . . . [O]nly if you're not too eager to proceed to other paragraphs will you get something out of it. People often race ahead without ever turning back and reflecting.
>
> . . . Still, once our intimate reading of it and careful reflection on it have led to a clear understanding of it, we must continue to question. Then there might be additional progress.

Confucian personal cultivation through full participation in ritual is not confined to the solemn "high" rituals of ancestral sacrifice, but is equally applicable in our everyday lives. Remember that the *li* include what we would call customs or manners, the importance of being polite and courteous expressed in culturally understood conventional ways. When we say "Good morning" to passersby on the street, or "Gesundheit " when someone sneezes, we are coming out of our personal shells, acknowledging the presence of other human beings, demonstrating fellow-membership in a cultural heritage, and much more. These "little rituals" so to speak, are no less the glue of our social interactions than weddings, bar mitzvahs, graduations, and funerals, for without them our social lives would be chaotic at best, brutal or cruel at worst. And just as with solemn rites, the little rituals we perform daily can be done well or poorly, warmly or coldly, clumsily or with grace and dignity. Think of the different ways we may shake hands when introduced to someone. We might not even extend our hand, but simply nod in the other's direction. Or we may hold out our hand perfunctorily, akin to putting a dead fish in the other's hand. Or we can show off our strength and ego by squeezing the other's hand until it hurts. Or finally, we might grasp the other's hand firmly but not harshly, perhaps enclosing them with our left hand, looking at the other directly, smiling and saying with sincerity, "I'm very pleased to meet you." It is for this reason that for Confucian personal cultivation, the spiritual discipline attendant on ritual does not merely prescribe our participation in rituals, we must practice them as well, until we are no longer self-conscious about their performance, and we have come to do them effortlessly and spontaneously, with grace, warmth, and dignity, celebrating the co-humanity of our fellow participants in a ritual, even the "little" ones.

If our lives are basically constituted by the others with whom we interact, if they are essential to our well-being and sense of who we are, then clearly rituals, great and small alike, have a major role to play in having us come to see, feel, understand that much of what we do contributes to the flourishing or degradation of others, just as the actions of others contribute so much to our flourishing, or degradation. We are all taught from very early on to say "Thank you" -- a little ritual --when someone does a kindness for us, but from a Confucian perspective, to say "Thank you" is also to give a gift; an acknowledgement that the other is a fellow human being, and one who has made a difference for the better, however slight, in our life.

There are, then, several dimensions to ritual involvement as a spiritual discipline. On the one hand it contributes to ego–reduction ("Not my will, but Thy will be done"), as we commit ourselves to be bound by the behavioral constraints the *li* impose on us, as we figuratively bow before the customs and traditions of the past, and literally bow before the physical symbols of our ancestors. At the same time, close attentiveness to the practice of rituals requires a discipline of its own, closely akin to the yogic disciplines many people now study and practice. Relatedly, the discipline of practicing rituals can lead to their performance spontaneously, with grace and beauty, and altogether unself-consciously. After years and years of practice and performance, the prima ballerina's dance is graceful, effortless, spontaneous; if she should think self–consciously even for an instant of where her feet should go next, the dance is over. And finally, for the Confucians the social dimensions of rituals are always at the forefront of their instructions, which contributes significantly to preparing the practitioner-performer of *li* for the religious experience of feeling at one with the ancestors, peers, and future generations, akin, perhaps, to the kind of thrill all but the most spiritually deadened or misanthropic among us feel, even if only briefly, when hearing the final movement of Beethoven's 9th Symphony, the "Ode to Joy." Of course we are moved deeply by the music, but also inspired by the words of Schiller's poem.

Chapter 13

SUMMARY SUGGESTIONS

A reader may surely come to feel comfortable with, and learn much from the *Analects* without ever following any of the suggestions for doing so that run through this little *Companion*. And almost as surely it would hinder befriending the book by attempting to follow all of them from the start. But some of the suggestions should be of some assistance to some people, others to others, and perhaps everyone should become acquainted with the students.

My recommendations are partially based on my own reading experiences of the text, others I developed for working with students and colleagues over the decades I have taught the *Analects*.; and still other suggestions were given to me by students and colleagues who came up with them on their own, and found them useful. In this concluding chapter I reiterate a few suggestions proffered in earlier chapters along with brief additional aids for working to make the text one's own.

In earlier chapters we have considered the importance of reading the *Analects* actively rather than passively, and both directly and indirectly; reading it closely and carefully, and charitably whenever possible: you may certainly come to reject some or much of the teachings found in the *Analects,* but always keep in mind the unlikelihood that a person regarded as a culture's most respected thinker for well over 2000 years is a fool.

Another parallel abstract suggestion I can proffer to help you the reader in approaching the text is to see it as both a window and a mirror, briefly mentioned in earlier chapters. It is a window onto a world far distant from us in time and space, and the more closely you endeavor to discern its features the more you can come to terms with what its most prominent figure and his followers might have been thinking and doing. And it is a mirror through which we all might well learn much about ourselves, certainly a central feature of the Master's teaching techniques with his students.

Actively Reading the Text as Window

I. When you come across an analect that does not seem to make sense, or is not at all in keeping with most others, there are a number of things you can do: 1) Read the analects immediately preceding and following the puzzling passage; at times, several of them are on the same or very similar topic. 2) Ask why or under what circumstances someone might say what the analect says – and do it sympathetically. 3) If the puzzling passage is a statement from Confucius, ask whether he might be making a joke, a pun, is being ironic, or making a statement intended strictly for the student to whom it is addressed (11.22 once more). 4) If the passage seems inconsistent with another, check (Ch. 2) the estimated age of the Books in which they are found. Also endeavor to think through the seeming inconsistency.

II. When you come across a topic or concept closely related to another, cross-reference them both in the margin of your text, and keep doing this as you come across additional passages on that topic or concept. (This also serves to give you the rudiments of a topical concordance; if you have a sense of the specific topic in an analect you are hunting for, finding any one of them on that topic can give you the others noted in the margin if you've done your cross-referencing regularly.)

III. Follow the method of **II**, only now cross-referencing biographical statements by the Master. You can do this for his autobiographical statements as well.

IV. More systematically, using your finding list, read all of the analects with or about one of the students in them *seriatim;* it should help give you a fair idea of who and what they were -- and what Confucius thought of them -- fairly early in your studies of the text.

V. You can check up on the tentative results you obtain in these efforts by consulting one or more of the appropriate reference works briefly described in the Bibliography below. Readers should not, however, abandon their interpretations too quickly if they do not square with what is found in one or another of the reference works; some of the latter will not square with each other either. Rather should the reader's interpretations first be re-thought, focusing especially on the evidence that determined them.

Actively Reading the Text As Mirror

VI. Reiterating some of the themes of the Chapter 6, after coming to a tentative evaluation of a particular student the reader should reflect on why that evaluation was made. That is to say, given that the textual evidence is mixed for all of them except Yan Hui, why did you weigh the positive (negative) evidence more favorably than the negative (positive)?

VII. After following **III,** above, the same question may be asked about Confucius. Given that there are differing accounts – at least in details – in the biographical passages in the *Analects,* which weighed most heavily on you the reader, and why? And the question may be asked yet again with respect to the *auto*biographical passages.

VIII. Still on the topic of coming to a perspective on the Master, the reader may/should ask whether the biographical evidence, autobiographical statements, and comments made to students form, or do not form, an integrated whole. Writing a 500-word biography of Confucius, based solely on the texts, can be an excellent way of coming to know your teacher better.

IX. Memorize some analects, especially those that have struck you as particularly important. Rote memorization has limits as a pedagogic technique, but within those limits it can be quite effective.

X. Open the text randomly occasionally, in the morning, and read carefully the passage on which your eye falls, reflecting on it when you can during the course of the day. This is definitely *not* to suggest the *Analects* be used as you might read the daily horoscope in the paper; it is to suggest a way of keeping the text near to mind when it cannot be near to hand.

XI. Take note of a passage you find outrageously mistaken. Then, at an appropriate moment with a colleague, friend or family member, defend the view advanced in that passage. In due course, with another such passage, repeat.

XII. Try writing an analect or two of your own. Don't strive for fortune cookie fame, work within the structure and tenor of the text.

Thus ends this little *Companion*, which I hope may "hold up one corner" (7.8) sufficient to be of help to my readers in learning how to hold up the other three for themselves. But to balance all my exhortations to read the text regularly, rigorously, and resolutely I want to let Zhu Xi have the final word:

> In a day you can only read so much, and your efforts have a limit as well. You mustn't want to do everything at once.

Chapter 14

A BIBLIOGRAPHIC ESSAY

A full bibliography on Confucius and the *Analects* would more than double the length of this book. Having to be selective of course entails being somewhat subjective as well, to which I must call attention but without apology; any selection of books must be at least somewhat personal no less than professional. I have listed a few works here, for example, that would no longer be found in most standard bibliographies because I believe the insights they contain remain valid, and I have omitted others because I do not believe they contain any genuine insights into the man or the text. There are, probably unfortunately for readers under 40, no electronic sources listed here, in part because I am highly challenged electronically and so do not employ them very much, and also because this whole work is about *books,* for which, again, I make no apologies. I have kept specialized works of scholarship to a minimum, as well as those that take up much more of the Confucian persuasion than simply its First Ancestor and the sayings attributed to him by his descendants. Hence there will be many omissions here which should *not* lead anyone to think I hold any of them in particular in low regard.

A Reader's Companion

Background/Reference Readings

As noted earlier, Confucius celebrated much of the history, rituals, customs and more, of the millennium that preceded him, and it is therefore valuable to learn more about his inherited tradition. Although two decades old now, *Heritage of China,* edited by Paul Ropp (Univ. of California Press, 1990), is a splendid introduction to the several dimensions of Chinese culture – religion, science, women and the family, economics, government, art, etc. –with each chapter written by a specialist in that dimension. The earliest documented period, the late Shang, is well described by David N. Keightley in his *The Ancestral Landscape* (Univ. of California Press, 2000). Although including much material far beyond Confucius himself and the *Analects,* an essential reference work for every serious student is the *RoutledgeCurzon Encyclopedia of Confucianism,* in two volumes (2003), edited by Xinzhong Yao. A topic close to Confucius, but with relatively little written about it, may be examined in the catalog accompanying a major archaeological exhibit at the Sackler Museum, *Music in the Age of Confucius,* edited by Jenny F. So, and published by the Smithsonian Institution in 2000. Readers will also profit from Reading Nathan Sivin's *Medicine, Philosophy & Religion in Ancient China,* published by Variorum in England in 1995. (The quotation from Sivin in Capter 8 is taken from this work, p. 328, n.46.)

Henry Rosemont, Jr.

The Classics

In the *Analects* a number of references are made to the *Book of Odes* and the *Book of History,* and according to at least a few scholars to the *Book of Changes (Yi Jing/I Ching))* as well. The tradition also accords him the editorship of other works, which, along with *The Records of Ritual,* later became "classics." A splendid summary account of each of these basic texts is Michael Nylan's *The Five "Confucian" Classics* (Random House/Doubleday, 2010). Four of these classics were well translated by James Legge (about whom, more below), and the most well-known of the translations of the fifth -- the *Book of Changes* -- is by Richard Wilhelm (Bollingen/Pantheon), first published in 1950 with numerous subsequent printings. *Caveat emptor* applies even more to books on the *Yi Jing* than to almost any other Chinese text, but another solid work is Richard John Lynn's *The Classic of Changes* (Columbia Univ. Press, 2004), in which the Wang Bi commentary is translated along with the text of the *Yi*. Finally, although fairly technical much of the time, Edward L. Shaughnessy's essays gathered in his *Before Confucius* (SUNY Press, 1997) show textual scholarship, philology and detective work all in play in attempting to get clearer about who compiled the ancient classics, when and why, and what they said, at least in part. Although not accorded the status of a "classic" until the Tang dynasty *The Chinese Classic of Family Reverence* was very influential for centuries before then. The most recent translation is another that Roger Ames and I have done together, published by the Univ. of Hawai'i Press in 2008. The short little work which largely records a (real or imagined) series of conversations between the Master and his student Zeng Zi, and expands significantly on the laconic remarks about the depth of importance of the family and interrelationality found in the *Analects*.

Philosophy & Religion

Herbert Fingarette's *Confucius – The Secular as Sacred*, published by Harper Torchbooks in 1972, can be seen as marking the rebirth of interest in Confucius as a major philosopher who has much to say today; it is essential reading for everyone in the field, and was re-issued by Waveland Press in 1998. A further boost to seeing Confucius as a major philosopher with contemporary lessons to teach came with *Thinking Through Confucius* by David L. Hall and Roger T. Ames, published by SUNY Press in 1987; it, too, is required reading for everyone wishing to deepen their knowledge of the Master and his ideas. The religious dimensions of Confucian thought throughout its history are described in a series of essays by noted scholars edited by Tu Weiming and Mary Evelyn Tucker, *Confucian Spirituality*, published by Crossroads Press in 2003; some of the essays focus on Confucius himself, and the *Analects*. A solid collection of essays on the man and the text by both senior and junior scholars, edited by Bryan W. Van Norden, was published by Oxford University Press in 2002, entitled *Confucius and the Analects*. The concluding essay by Joel Sahleen is a bibliography of works on the subject(s) that is fairly comprehensive through 1998. Two other collections of scholarly essays on the Master and the book are due to appear in 2014. First is *The Norton Critical Edition of the Analects*, edited by Michael Nylan (Norton. The & Co.), and the other is *The Dao Companion to the Analects*, edited by Amy Olberding, being published by Springer Press. A little and little-known book by Edward Herbert, whom Arthur Waley described as "an informed summarizer of specialist knowledge" is *A Confucian Notebook*, first published in the U.S. by Grove Press in 1960.

Biographies

One reason that there are relatively few biographies of Confucius in English, given his fame and stature, is the paucity of reliable sources on which they might be based. One source would be the *Analects* itself, plus remarks about him in the *Zuo Commentary* classic, not too distant in time from much of the *Analects* (i.e., within a century of the Master's death). The other major source of material before the Common Era is the lengthy biography written by the historian Sima Qian five centuries after Confucius died, published in his *Historical Records*. Everything else demands detective work and informed utilization of other materials. Two recent biographies may be distinguished, at least in part, by which source is seen as basic by the author and which as secondary. In *The Authentic Confucius* (Scribner, 2007), Annping Chin opts for the earlier source(s), and it is a solid work in spite of its rather presumptuous title. Relying more closely on Sima Qian, fellow historians Michael Nylan and

Thomas Wilson generally follow his lead, and use the *Analects* and the *Zuo Commentary* as corroborative and supplemental, and like Chin use other materials judiciously as well. *The Lives of Confucius,* however (Random House/Doubleday, 2010), goes well beyond the life of the man himself, treating in detail how that life was seen and described, and his views amended, throughout later Chinese history, and into the present, giving the reader a panoramic view of the different ways the Master has been interpreted over the centuries. The work is very well done in my view; to declare interests however, I must note that I have been included in the final chapter as a representative of contemporary Confucian scholarship in the West. An excellent companion to the second half of *Lives of Confucius* – which takes up his portrayals in later imperial Chinese history – is *Confucius: His Life and Legacy in Art,* the catalog of an exhibition at the China Institute in New York, edited by Lu Wensheng and Julia K. Murray, published in 2009. An older biography, but a good one, is H.G. Creel, *Confucius and the Chinese Way* (Harper Torchbooks, 1960). The same may be said for Shigeki Kaizuka's *Confucius: His Life and Thought.* Long out of print, it was reprinted by Dover Books in 2002; an excellent example of Japanese scholarship on Confucius. The Englishman, Jonathan Clements – a dilettante in the English sense of the term – published *Confucius* (Sutton Pub., Ltd., 2004), which strings together almost every legend about the life and ancestry of Confucius ever recorded. It is entertaining, but not reliable reading. Another work, which is a "biography" of Chinese civilization interwoven with that of Confucius, is *Confucius: Making the Way Great,* by Ni Peimin. A handsome little book with many illustrations, it was published by the Shanghai Translation Publishing House in 2010. To understand the vilification the shade of the Master endured during the "Anti-Lin Biao, Anti-Confucius" campaign of the Great Proletarian Cultural Revolution for the first half of the 1970s, Yang Jung-Kuo's *Confucius: "Sage" of the Reactionary Classes* (Peking Foreign Languages Press, 1974) is essential reading. This text can then be compared with Yu Dan's *Confucius from the Heart*, of which well over ten million copies have been sold (or pirated), with perhaps as many as two million of them distributed in the countryside by the Chinese government. An English translation was made available by Atria Books in 2009, but readers must be warned that the book, like Yang's, should be read for what it says about the China of the period, NOT for what it accurately tells us about Confucius or the *Analects,* which is not much, in my view.

Translations

NOTE: After the translator's name, [P] indicates *pinyin* Romanization was used, [WG] Wade-Giles, and [O] is simply "other."

Beginning with our own, the full citation for A&R is Roger T. Ames and Henry Rosemont, Jr. [P], *The Analects of Confucius: A Philosophical Translation* (Random House/Ballantine, 1998).

Other competent translations with components to recommend them are those by Arthur Waley [WG], an older but very well-written translation most recently re-issued by Vintage in 1989; Raymond Dawson's [P] translation has a number of interesting notes at the end of the text; the well-known D.C. Lau [WG] (Penguin, 1979) has brought his considerable skills to bear on his translation, even though he would make Confucius more akin to a Western moral philosopher than I would (ditto for his otherwise very good translation of Mencius); although much older, William Soothill's [WG] translation still has merit, and thanks to being reprinted by Dover, can be purchased for $3.00, a bargain; a newer translation by Edward Slingerland [P] is solid, and has the virtue of also including selections from some Chinese commentaries on the text (Hackett Pub. Co., 2003). The translation by Huang Chichung [P] has its fans, and he provides notes for virtually all of the 511 analects as they appear (Oxford University Press, 1997). Columbia University Press published the prodigious Burton Watson's translation [P] in 2010, which briefly identifies most of the people (not alone students) mentioned in the text. Simon Leys [P] (Norton, 1997) uses colloquial English very well most of the time, but thereby takes some liberties with the text, as does David Hinton's [WG] more poetic translation, elegantly composed, published by Counterpoint in 1999.

The Original Analects by Bruce and Taeko Brooks [**O**] (Columbia Univ. Press, 2001) is in a class by itself, an effort to place the 20 books and 511 sayings that comprise the text in chronological order with great precision. The philological, historical and logical methods displayed are impressive; it is a great work of scholarship even though the conclusions reached by the translators have not been widely accepted in the field. The translation is competent, but in my view lacks the zestfulness reflected in many of the exchanges between the Master and the student(s). The Romanization system is unique, making reading difficult at times. It is nevertheless a work of great scholarship that must eventually be on the shelf of every serious student of the *Analects*.

Confucius, by Ezra Pound [**O**], also stands by itself. Highly idiosyncratic, it nevertheless captures well the spirit as well as the letter of the text at times in my opinion, even though it does not accomplish either at other times. It was published by New Directions in 1969, and includes the Chinese text, plus a translation of the "Great Learning" and the "Doctrine of the Mean" as well (which titles Pound translates as "Great Digest" and "The Unwobbling Pivot" respectively).

A partial translation of the *Analects,* and the *Mencius,* with full translations of the other two shorter texts also translated by Pound, above, as "The Great Learning" and "Maintaining Perfect Balance," was ably done by Daniel Gardner [**P**], and published by Hackett in 2007 under the title *The Four Books: The Basic Teachings of the Later Confucian Tradition*. These texts were selected by Zhu Xi as representing the essence of Confucian teachings, and were required reading for all budding scholars and officials in China for 700 years. Although Zhu Xi was, in my view, sufficiently steeped in Buddhism to make his interpretation of the Confucius of the *Analects* more a metaphysician than I should like, he should definitely be studied carefully after readers of the *Analects* have formed an initial opinion of the book on their own, and Gardner has done much to make his thinking accessible. I recommend highly another translation of his on Zhu Xi published by the University of California Press in 1990, Learning To Be a Sage (from which the several brief quotes on reading in this Companion have been taken, from the section "On Reading," Part I, pp.128-142)), and *Zhu xi's Reading of the Analects* (Columbia University Press, 2003).

Finally, the work of James Legge [O]. Although some of his translations were done almost a century and a half ago, they all remain required reading for students of China's classical period. Thus his translation should be the second every student of the Analects should buy in my opinion but it is his The Chinese Classics, especially Volume I, that the student should purchase, not one of the numerous translations of the Analects that now appear because his work is in the public domain; most of these works do not contain the Chinese text, the copious footnotes and commentary, or the comprehensive introductions to the text, including brief accounts of 86 students of Confucius, as found in Volume I. The Chinese Classics has been published in both five and seven volume editions over a lengthy period of time, and pieces of them are available online now. His system of

Romanization takes time to become familiar, but is not singular, as Pound followed him orthographically.

APPENDIX I:

Transcription Conversion Table

Table 1

Pinyin	Wade-Giles
a	a
b	p
c	ts',tz'
ch	ch'
d	t
e	e
g	k
i	yi
j	ch
k	k'
o	e *or* o
p	p'

q	ch
r	j
si	ssu,szu
t	t'
x	hs
yi	i
yu	u, yu
you	yu
z	ts,tz
zh	ch
zi	tzu
-i (zhi)	-ih (chih)
-ie (lie)	-ieh (lieh)
-r (er)	rh (erh)

Examples

Pinyin	Wade-Giles
jiang	chiang
zhiang	ch'iang
zi	tzu
zhi	chih
cai	tsai
Zu Xi	Chu Hsi
Xunzi	Hsün Tzu
qing	ch'ing
xue	hsüeh

Table 2

Wade-Giles	Pinyin
a	a
ch'	ch
ch	j
ch	q
ch	zh
e	e
e *or* o	o
f	f
h	h
hs	x
i	yi
-ieh (lieh)	-ie (lie)
-ih (chih)	-I (zhi)
j	r
k	g
k'	k
p	b
p'	p
rh (erh)	-r (er)

ssu, szu	si
t	d
t'	t
ts', tz'	c
ts, tz	z
tzu	zi
u, yu	u
yu	you

Examples

Wade-Giles	**Pinyin**
chiang	jiang
ch'iang	zhiang
ch'ing	qing
chih	zhi
Chu Hsi	Zhu Xi
hsüeh	xue
Hsün Tzu	Xunzi
tsai	cai
tzu	zi

APPENDIX II

Concordance of Key Philosophical Terms

爱 *ai* (to love)
1.5, 1.6, 3.17, 12.10, 12.22, 14.7, 17.4, 17.21 (9)

道 *dao* (Way, path, road, *The* Way, to tread a path, to speak, doctrines, etc.)
1.2, 1.5, 1.11, 1.12, 1.14, 1.15, 2.3, 3.16, 3.24, 4.5, 4.8, 4.9, 4.15, 4.20, 5.2, 5.7, 5.13, 5.16, 5.21, 6.12, 6.17, 6.24, 7.6, 8.4, 8.7, 8.13, 9.12, 9.27, 9.30, 11.20, 11.24, 12.19, 12.23, 13.25, 14.1, 14.3, 14.19, 14.28, 14.36, 15.7, 15.25, 15.29, 15.32, 15.40, 15.42, 16.2, 16.5, 16.11, 17.4, 17.14, 18.2, 18.5, 18.7, 19.2, 19.4, 19.7, 19.12, 19.19, 19.22, 19.25. (90)

德 *de* (Virtue, Power, Excellence)
1.9, 2.1, 2.3, 4.11, 4.25, 6.29, 7.3, 7.6, 7.23, 8.1, 8.20, 9.18, 11.3, 12.10, 12.19, 12.21, 13.22, 14.4, 14.5, 14.33, 14.34, 15.4, 15.13, 15.27, 16.1, 16.12, 17.13, 17.14, 18.5, 19.2, 19.11. (40)

鬼神 *gui shen* (Ghosts and spirits)
2.24, 3.12, 6.22, 7.21, 7.35, 8.21, 11.12 (9)

和 *he* ("Harmony")
1.12, 7.32, 13.23, 16.1, 19.25. (8)

家 *jia* (Family, Home)
3.2, 5.8, 12.2, 12.20, 16.1, 17.18, 19.23, 19.25 (11)

諫 *jian* (Remonstrance, to remonstrate)
3.21, 4.18, 18.1, 18.5, 19.10 (5)

教 *jiao* (teachings, to instruct)
2.20, 7.25, 13.9, 13.29, 13.30, 15.39, 20.2 (7)

敬 *jing* (Respect, respectfully, reverence,)
1.5, 2.7, 2.20, 3.26, 4.18, 5.16, 5.17, 6.2, 6.22, 8.4, 11.15, 12.5, 13.4, 13.19, 14.42, 15.6, 15.33, 15.38, 16.10, 19.1 (22)

君子 *junzi*

(Exemplary persons, Gentleman, Superior man, Noble Man)
1.1, 1.2, 1.8, 1.14, 2.12, 2.13, 2.14, 3.5, 3.7, 3.24, 4.5, 4.10, 4.11, 4.16, 4.24, 5.3, 5.16, 6.4, 6.13, 6.18, 6.26, 6.27, 7.26, 7.31, 7.33, 7.37, 8.2, 8.4, 8.6, 9.6, 9.14, 10.6, 11.1, 11.21, 11.26, 12.4, 12.5, 12.8, 12.16, 12.19, 12.24, 13.3, 13.23, 13.25, 13.26, 14.6, 14.23, 14.26, 14.27, 14.28,

14.42, 15.2, 15.7, 15.18, 15.19, 15.20, 15.21, 15.22, 15.23, 15.32, 15.34, 15.37, 16.1, 16.6, 16.7, 16.8, 16.10, 16.13, 17.4, 17.7, 17.21, 17.23, 17.24, 18.7, 18.10, 19.3, 19.4, 19.7, 19.9, 19.10, 19.12, 19.20, 19.21, 19.25, 20.2, 20.3 (108)
(NOTE: 君 *also occurs alone 40+ times in the text, where it means "lord," or "ruler"*)

禮 *li* (Ritual propriety, Rituals, Rites, Customs, Worship, Ceremony, etc.)
1.12, 1.13, 1.15, 2.3, 2.5, 2.23, 3.4, 3.8, 3.9, 3.15, 3.17, 3.18, 3.19, 3.22, 3.26, 4.13, 6.27, 7.18, 7.31, 8.2, 8.8, 9.3, 9.11, 10.5, 11.1, 11.26, 12.1, 12.5, 12.15, 13.3, 13.4, 14.12, 14.41, 15.18, 15.33, 16.2, 16.5, 16.13, 17.11, 17.21, 17.24, 20.3. (75)

命 *ming* (Destiny, Fate, Mandate, Propensities)
2.4, 6.3, 6.10, 8.6, 9.1, 10.3, 10.20, 11.7, 11.19, 12.5, 13.20, 14.8, 14.12, 14.36, 14.44, 16.2, 16.8, 17.20, 19.1, 20.1, 20.3 (24)

仁 *ren* (Authoritative, Benevolence, Human-heartedness, Consummate conduct, etc)
1.2, 1.3, 1.6, 3.3, 4.1, 4.2, 4.3, 4.4, 4.5, 4.6, 4.7, 5.5, 5.8, 5.9, 5.19, 6.7, 6.22, 6.23, 6.26, 6.30, 7.6, 7.15, 7.30, 7.34, 8.2, 8.7, 8.10, 9.1, 9.29, 12.1,

12.2, 12.3, 12.20, 12.22, 12.24, 13.12, 13.19, 13.27, 14.1, 14.4, 14.6, 14.16, 14.17, 14.28, 15.9, 15.10, 15.33, 15.35, 15.36, 17.1, 17.6, 17.8, 17.17, 17.21, 18.1, 19.6, 19.15, 19.16, 20.1, 20.2. (109)

善 *shan* (Almost always rendered as "Good," but the sense of the term is more "good for," "good at," i.e, having the ability, useful, a worthy example of things of this kind, etc.)
2.220, 3.25, 5.17, 5.26, 6.9, 7.3, 7.22, 7.26, 7.28, 7.32, 8.4, 8.13, 9.11, 9.13, 11.20, 12.11, 12.19, 12.21, 12.23, 13.8, 13.11, 13.15, 13.22, 13.24, 13.29, 14.5, 15.10, 15.33, 16.4, 16.5, 16.11, 17.7, 19.3, 19.20, 20.1 (42)

聖 (人) *sheng (ren)* (Sage(s), saint)
6.30, 7.26, 7.34, 9.6, 16.8, 19.12 (8)

士 *shi* (Scholar-apprentice, lower official, knight, retainer)
4.9, 7.12, 8.7, 12.20, 13.20, 13.28, 14.2, 15.9-10, 18.2, 18.6, 18.11, 19., 19.19 (18)

恕 *shu* (to reciprocate, reciprocity, forgiveness, mercy)
4.15, 15.24 (2)

天 *tian* ("Heaven," "Nature")
2.4, 3.2, 3.11, *3.13*, *3.24*, 4.10, *5.13*, *6.28*, *7.23*, 8.1, 8.13, 8.18, *8.19*, 8.20, *9.5*, *9.6*, *11.9*, 12.1, *12.5*, 12.22, 14.5, 14.17, *14.35*, 16.2, *16.8*, 17.6, *17.19*, 17.21, 19.20, *19.25*, *20.1*. (49)
NOTE: Only the italicized numbers refer to passages with 天 occurring as such; all other passages are 天下, "All under heaven," i.e. "the world.")

文 *wen*
(Culture, Refined, Literature, to embellish, etc.)
1.6, 3.9, 3.14, 5.13, 5.15, 5.18, 5.19, 5.20, 6.18, 6.27, 7.25, 7.33 8.19, 9.5, 9.11, 11.3, 12.8, 12.15, 12.24, 14.12, 14.13, 14.15, 14.18, 15.14, 15.26, 16.1, 19.8, 19.22. (42)

孝 *xiao* (Filial piety, Family Reverence)
1.2, 1.6, 1.11, 2.5, 2.6, 2.7, 2.8, 2.20, 2.21, 4.20, 8.21, 11.5, 13.20, 19.18 (19)

小人 *xiao ren* (Petty person, Mean person)
2.14, 4.11, 4.16, 6.13, 7.37, 12.16, 12.19, 13.4, 13.20, 13.23, 13.25, 13.26, 14.6, 14.23, 15.2, 15.21, 15.34, 16.8, 17.4, 17.12, 17.23, 17.25, 19.8. (23)

信 *xin* (Making good on one's word, Trustworthy, Sincere, authentic, etc.)
1.4, 1.5, 1.6, 1.7, 1.8, 1.13, 2.22, 5.6, 5.10, 5.26, 5.28, 7.1, 7.25, 8.4, 8.13, 8.16, 9.25, 12.7, 12.10, 12.11, 13.4, 13.20, 14.13, 14.14, 14.31, 15.6, 15.18, 17.6, 17.8, 19.2, 19.10, 20.1. (38)

心 *xin* (Heart, mind, heart-mind)
2.4, 6.7, 14.39, 17.22, 20.1 (6)

学 *xue* (Learning, to learn, studying)
1.1, 1.6, 1.7, 1.8, 1.14, 2.4, 2.15, 2.18, 5.15, 5.28, 6.3, 6.27, 7.2, 7.3, 7.17, 7.34, 8.12, 8.13, 8.17, 9.2, 9.30, 11.3, 11.7, 11.25, 11.26, 12.15, 13.4, 14.24, 14.35, 15.1, 15.3, 15.312, 15.32, 16.9, 16.13, 17.4, 17.8, 17.9, 19.5, 19.6, 19.7, 19.13, 19.22. (65)

義 *yi* (Right, Righteous, Moral, Appropriate)
1.13, 2.24, 4.10, 4.16, 5.16, 6.22, 7.3, 7.16, 12.10, 12.20, 13.4, 14.12, 14.13, 15.17, 15.18, 16.10, 16.11, 17.23, 18.7, 19.1. (24)

勇 *yong* (bold, daring, brave, courageous)
2.24, 5.7, 8.2, 8.10, 9.29, 11.24, 14.4, 14.12, 14.28, 17.7, 17.21, 17.22 (16)

政 *zheng* (Government, To govern, lead)
1.10, 2.1, 2.3, 2.21, 4.13, 5.19, 6.8, 8.14, 11.3, 12.7, 12.11, 12.14, 12.17, 12.19, 13.1, 13.2, 13.5, 13.7, 13.13, 13.14, 13.16, 13.17, 13.20, 14.26, 16.2, 16.3, 18.5, 19.18, 20.1, 20.2. (43)

正 *zheng* (to correct, rectify, make proper)
1.14, 7.34, 8.4, 9.15, 10.8, 10.12, 10.18, 10.26, 12.17, 13.3, 13.6, 13.13, 14.15, 15.5, 17.10, 20.2 (24)

忠 *zhong* (Loyalty, Obedience,)
1.4, 1.8, 2.20, 3.19, 4.15, 5.19, 5.28, 7.25, 9.25, 12.10, 12.14, 12.23, 13.19, 14.7, 15.6, 16.10. (18)

知 *zhi* (Realize, realization, to realize; Knowledge, Wisdom, Acknowledge,)
1.1, 1.12, 1.15, 1.16, 2.4, 2.11, 2.17, 2.22, 2.23, 3.11, 3.15, 3.22, 3.23, 4.1, 4.2, 4.7, 4.14, 4.21, 5.5, 5.8, 5.9, 5.18, 5.19, 5.21, 5.22, 6.20, 6.22, 6.23, 7.14, 7.19, 7.20, 7.28, 7.31, 8.3, 8.9, 8.16, 9.6, 9.8, 9.23, 9.28, 9.29, 11.12, 11.26, 12.22, 13.2, 13.3, 13.15, 14.1, 14.12, 14.17, 14.28, 14.30, 14.35, 14.38, 14.39, 15.4, 15.8, 15.14, 15.19, 15.33, 15.34, 16.8, 16.9, 17.1, 17.3, 17.8, 17.24, 18.6, 18.7, 19.5, 19.24, 19.25, 20.3. (118)

APPENDIX III:

Student Finding List

(Includes all 15 students who appear 3 or more times in the text)

Fan Chi   2:5, 6:22, 12:21, 12:22, 13:4, 13:19

Gongxi Zihua   5:8, 6:4, 7:34, 11:26

Master You   1:2, 1:12, 1:13, 12:9

Master Zeng   1:4, 1:9, 4:15, 8:3-8:7 11:18, 12:24, 14:26, 19:17—19::19

Min Ziqian   6:9, 11:3, 11:5, 11:13, 11:14

Nanrong   5:2, 11:6, 14.5

Ran You   3:6, 5:8, 6:4, 6:8, 6:12, 7:15, 11:3, 11:13, 11:17, 11:22, 11:24, 11:26,   13:9, 13:14, 14:12, 16:1

Yan Hui   5:26, 6:7, 6:11, 7:11, 8:5, 9:11, 9:20—9:21, 11:3, 11:4, 11:7—11:11, 11:19, 11:23, 12:1, 15:11

Zai Wo   3:21, 5:10, 6:26, 11:3, 17:21

Zhonggong   5.5,   6:1, 6:2, 6:6, 11:3, 12:2, 13:2

Zigong   1:10, 1:15, 2:13, 3:17, 5:4, 5:9, 5:13, 5:15, 6:8, 6:30, 7:15, 9:6, 9:13, 11:3, 11:13, 11:16, 11:19,   12:7, 12:8, 12:23, 13:20, 13:24, 14:17, 14:28, 14:29, 14:35, 15:3, 15:10, 15:24, 17:19, 17:24, 19:20—19:25

Zilu   2:17, 5:7, 5:8, 5:14, 5:26, 6:8, 6:28, 7:11, 7:19, 7:35, 9:12, 9:27, 11:3, 11:13, 11:15, 11:18, 11:22, 11:24, 11:25, 11:26, 12:12, 13:1, 13:3, 13:28, 14:12, 14:16, 14:22, 14:36, 14:42, 15:2, 15:4, 16:1, 17:5, 17:7, 17:8, 17:23, 18:6, 18:7

Zixia   1:7, 2:8, 3:8, 6:13, 11:3, 11:16, 12:5, 12:22, 13:17, 19:3—19:13

Ziyou   2:7, 4:26, 6:14, 11:3, 17:4, 19:12, 19:14, 19:15

Zi Zhang   2:18, 2:23, 5:19, 11:16, 11:18, 11:20, 12:6, 12:10, 12:14, 12:20, 14:40, 15:6, 15:42, 17:6, 19:1—19:3, 19:15, 19:16, 20:2

ABOUT THE AUTHOR

Henry Rosemont, Jr. is a philosopher who has written *A Chinese Mirror, Rationality and Religious Experience,* and, with Huston Smith, *Is there a Universal Grammar of Religion?* With Roger Ames he has translated *The Analects of Confucius* and *The Chinese Classic of Family Reverence,* and with Daniel Cook, *Leibniz: Writings on China.* He has edited several other volumes, including *Explorations in Chinese Cosmology* and *Chinese Texts and Philosophical Contexts.* He has taught at St. Mary's College of Maryland, Johns Hopkins – SAIS, and Fudan University in Shanghai. For the last decade he has held various appointments in the Religious Studies Department at Brown, currently as a Visiting Scholar.